Biblical and Ancient Greek Linguistics

Volume 4 — 2015

Contents

Biblical and Ancient Greek Linguistics (*BAGL*) is an international journal that exists to further the application of modern linguistics to the study of Ancient and Biblical Greek, with a particular focus on the analysis of texts, including but not restricted to the Greek New Testament. The journal is hosted by McMaster Divinity College and works in conjunction with its Centre for Biblical Linguistics, Translation and Exegesis and the OpenText.org organization (www.opentext.org) in the sponsoring of conferences and symposia open to scholars and students researching in Greek linguistics who are interested in contributing to advancing the discussion and methods of the field of research. *BAGL* is a refereed on-line and print journal dedicated to distributing the results of significant research in the area of linguistic theory and application to biblical and ancient Greek, and is open to all scholars, not just those connected to the Centre and the OpenText.org project. Accepted pieces are in the first instance posted on-line in page-consistent pdf format, and then (except for reviews) are published in print form each volume year. This format ensures timely posting of the most recent work in Greek linguistics with consistently referencable articles then available in permanent print form.

Submissions to BAGL

BAGL accepts submissions in five categories, and manuscripts are to be labeled as such at the time of submission:

Articles
Explorations
Notes
Responses
Reviews/Review articles

Submissions should follow the *BAGL* style-guide which can be found at http://bagl.org, and should include an abstract, not longer than 100 words, two to six keywords, and identification of the type of article (which will be noted at the time of posting and publication). Submissions not following the style-guide will be returned to the author for revision before being considered by the editors. Submissions should be sent in electronic form (Word or RTF) to Stanley E. Porter at princpl@mcmaster.ca. Assessment and response will be made within approximately two months of submission. Accepted submissions should be posted online within two months of acceptance.

The online form of *BAGL* is found at http://bagl.org.

ISBN 13: 978-1-4982-9544-4
www.wipfandstock.com
Manufactured in the U.S.A.

[*BAGL* 4 (2015) 5–6]

Editor's Foreword

Stanley E. Porter
McMaster Divinity College, Hamilton, ON, Canada

Publication of this volume of *Biblical and Ancient Greek Linguistics* (*BAGL*) brings our fourth volume year of publication to a close. We are already in the process of typesetting and then posting the several articles that we have accepted for volume 5 in 2016.

When we launched this peer-reviewed journal, we did not know what the results of such an attempt might be. We know that the number of scholars working in biblical and ancient Greek linguistics is relatively small compared to those working in other areas of biblical and ancient language studies. We hoped to be able to encourage those working in the field by hosting a journal dedicated to the subject. We also realize, however, that many of those scholars working in other areas have not yet been exposed to the kinds of discussions often held by biblical linguists. Some of these scholars might simply observe from the outside, but we had hopes that the journal might prompt others to enter into the discussion by submitting their own contributions. We wanted to provide an opportunity for fresh and innovative studies to be presented to a wider audience, regardless of one's previous orientation to Greek linguistics. Our hope, therefore, was twofold: to expand the scope and depth of the field of ancient Greek linguistic studies and to open this field up to a wider range of scholars.

The results have been encouraging and have begun to accomplish the goals that we set. We have established an excellent editorial board with a representative cross-section of interests and expertise. Members of the board, as well as some outside reviewers who have on occasion been called upon, have offered timely and incisive comments upon the work submitted for review. The format of the journal has allowed us to post articles of varying sizes. These sizes have ranged, so far, from our shortest article of six pages to our longest article of 55 pages. We have also had several other articles of about forty pages. (I note in anticipation that we may have several even longer articles in future volumes.) As a result, we have published seventeen articles in the first four volumes, with a minimum of four articles in each volume, along with complete indexes of both ancient sources and modern authors. These articles have been written by eleven different authors. The indexes provide an extra level of usefulness for searching our articles not usually found in other journals.

The range of subjects that we have treated so far in the four volumes is surprisingly wide. This fourth volume is the closest that we have come to a thematic issue. The first three articles all originated in a session on the sociolinguistics of early Christianity, using Acts 21:27–40 as a test case, organized by the New Testament Greek Language and Exegesis consultation of the Evangelical Theological Society in 2014. Sociolinguistics has probably been the most popular topic discussed in *BAGL* so far, but this is by accident rather than by intention. Other articles in the first four years have included studies of saliency, information flow, lexicography, Greek pedagogy, appraisal theory, monosemy, lexical priming, cross-linguistic grammar, Systemic Functional Linguistics, and a variety of others. There are a number of obvious topics that we have yet to address in our published articles. We are already anticipating greater diversity in both topics and contributors in forthcoming issues.

We are pleased with the current status of the journal, but are optimistic for its future and hope that an expanding number of scholars representing varied linguistic perspectives on biblical and other forms of ancient Greek will find the journal a suitable venue for publication.

[*BAGL* 4 (2015) 7–29]

Society and Culture: Aspects of the First-Century World for a More Contextually Driven Exegesis

Joseph D. Fantin
Dallas Theological Seminary, Dallas, TX, USA

Abstract: It is agreed that both context and Greek studies are essential components of the exegetical process. This article explores the function of language itself within society. The focus is not on the typical "meaning" of language as an information carrier but rather on the *meaning* that the use of particular linguistic elements brings to the communication situation. In other words, I will consider language itself as a social phenomenon. In order to achieve this goal, using Acts 21:27–40 as a test case, I will first consider selective elements of the social and historical context that when understood will contribute to recreating the context of the passage (cognitive environment). Then, with this contextual information activated in the exegetical process, I will consider the social impact of this information on two recorded speech incidents from Acts 21:27–40 resulting in a better understanding of the passage. This will demonstrate that in addition to the informational linguistic meaning, an understanding of the social use of language itself is a valuable tool for understanding the biblical text. (Article)

Keywords: Acts 21:27–40, exegesis, sociolinguistics, pragmatics, New Testament backgrounds, New Testament contexts, cognitive environment, Greek, relevance theory.

1. *Introduction*

Context! Context! Context! the old adage goes. In order to understand the Bible you must understand its context.[1] Often in

1. This is a revised version of a paper given in the New Testament

popular circles this has simply meant that one must read a passage of the Bible from within its larger literary context in the specific book. However, in more nuanced applications such as academic work or even in serious Bible study, context has come to include the historical, social, cultural, religious, etc., contexts of the author and his world. Often this information is labelled "backgrounds"; however, such a term seems to suggest that somehow this information is behind the Bible and that the Bible stands separate from it. The label "contexts" is preferred. This is a better way of describing this content because the Bible was written from *within* this sphere and is intimately connected with it.[2]

In my academic work I have become more and more convinced that an essential aspect of understanding the biblical text involves an attempt at reconstructing the original context, the cognitive environment,[3] of a specific book. We wish to get, so-to-speak, into the *sandals* of the original readers. I understand that such a task is impossible to fully accomplish for a number of reasons; however, the acknowledgment of this as a goal and the realization of the difficulty involved results in constraints on one's interpretation (what was not possibly understood in the original context cannot be the meaning today) and a certain humility about one's findings. Further, the objection that the impossibility of the task demands that it be abandoned is not worth entertaining. For it is better to knowingly use limited

Greek Language and Exegesis session at the national meeting of the Evangelical Theological Society, 19 November 2014 in San Diego. I would like to express my appreciation to Stanley Porter for inviting me to participate in this session and to all in attendance for helpful comments about the paper. Further I wish to thank my interns for the 2014–2015 school year, Jeremy Closs, Andrew Cress, and Lance Woodley, for help with putting the finishing touches on this paper. Andrew Cress was especially helpful by thoroughly proof-reading the article and helping transform it from an oral paper to a written article.

2. See Engberg-Pedersen, "Introduction," 1–2.

3. For a discussion of *cognitive environment* and its use in historical and exegetical work, see Fantin, *The Lord of the Entire Word*, 17–18. My view of the concept, cognitive environment, is influenced by Blakemore, *Relevance and Linguistic Meaning*, 69 and especially Sperber and Wilson, *Relevance*, 38–46.

knowledge about the ancient world while always being open to adjustments based on new learning and findings than it is to simply approach the text from a modern worldview. The latter has failed before it has even begun.[4]

The use of Greek has been an essential tool in exegesis for centuries. For some, this is the most important tool available. It is difficult to argue with this since Greek was the original language of our New Testament. It has been and remains the centerpiece of exegesis and is essential in much quality preaching and teaching. However, our understanding of Greek can unintentionally be influenced significantly by other factors such as our understanding of our own native language, Latin, or even modern Greek.

It may be preferable to view learning Greek as an aspect of the ancient context. It is not an isolated language element in the exegesis process but rather it is an essential part of reconstructing the cognitive environment. In other words, knowledge of Greek is one aspect of a reconstructed cognitive environment of the biblical communicators.

This article intends to be an exercise in just this, using the Greek language as a means of better understanding the original context. However, the focus will not be as much on Greek in the traditional manner, namely, syntactical classification, etc. This of course is a vital aspect of the process of understanding the cognitive environment. However, this cannot be our focus here. Rather, the focus will be on the use of language as a social phenomenon itself, not the content of the language (i.e., the meaning of the text). It is the use of language itself as a social tool that will enable us to understand the implied meaning of the text in a more nuanced manner.

After discussing some preliminary matters, Acts 21:27–40 will be used to help demonstrate the value of such information

4. Concerning using contextual information in the exegetical process, see Fantin, "Background Studies," 167–96.

for understanding the biblical text. This will not be a full exegetical treatment of this passage. Rather, our focus will be on the *use* of language with other aspects of the context considered as deemed necessary.

2. *Language as a Social Phenomenon*

There are many uses of language. We often do not consider this when using it. However, in addition to communicating propositional meaning, language can be used to comfort, frighten, assure, motivate, etc. Many might respond by stating that this is obvious and note that when one is sad, a comforting statement such as *It is okay* fits within our use of propositional language. Agreed. However, not all comforting is so linguistically transparent. For example, a child sitting on a playground crying because another child pushed him off a swing may be comforted by his mother with words such as *Let's go to the slide, Now that's really fun*, or *That child is a big bully*, or *Let's go home and have some ice cream*. These statements all communicate some sort of propositional message to the child; however, if we only assumed this meaning, we would probably miss the most important aspect of the communicative contribution, namely, comfort. There may have been no intention prior to this event to give the child ice cream. However, present circumstances demand a response of comfort that the mother feels appropriate for this situation. If successful, her words accomplish this.

There are many other uses of language that go beyond the transference of propositional information. Words can be used as physical art; an important aspect of poetry is the beauty of the sounds being enunciated, etc. This article will explore another use of language that goes beyond simple information transfer.

Before proceeding, it is worth noting that communication itself is not limited to language. Language is an essential element of most communication situations but is not required for communication to occur. One can communicate much with the point of a finger, a glance, a movement, etc. Thus communication is broader than language. As for language, the old code model of communication where one has a concept in one's mind, encodes it, sends it to another through language, and then the receiver decodes the language contribution with the result of a transfer of the information[5] does not hold up to scrutiny.[6] Rather, through the work of Paul Grice and then others such as Dan Sperber and Deirdre Wilson, it has been demonstrated that communication occurs primarily through inference.[7] The need for this approach can be easily demonstrated. For example, the so-called literal or code model approach without an incredibly bloated collection of linguistic "add-ons"[8] is unable to handle statements such as *I have nothing to wear to the party* and *You must be 21 to enter the pub*. These can be interpreted as one not having any clothes at all or that people only 21 year of age can enter the pub (i.e., not 20 years old or 22 years old, etc.). By contrast, an inferential approach often associated with pragmatics includes aspects of communication such as intention, implication, etc. Thus, language-proper linguistic code is one of a number of elements that must be interpreted to understand a communicative contribution. In the case of the two statements above, the hearer shares a cognitive environment with the speaker thus permitting the speaker to use his or her words more economically. Each statement is understood as *I have nothing* appropriate *to wear to the party* and *You must be* at least 21 years of age *to enter the pub*.[9]

5. See Fantin, *Greek Imperative Mood*, 43–49.

6. See the discussion in Fantin, *Greek Imperative Mood*, 43–60.

7. See Grice, "Logic and Conversation," 41–58; Grice, "Further Notes," 113–27; Sperber and Wilson, *Relevance*. For a discussion of the contribution these and other have made, see Fantin, *Greek Imperative Mood*, 43–65.

8. By "add-ons" I mean linguistic rules, etc., that are added on top of basic linguistic analysis. In practice one starts with a theory that explains straightforward, so-called literal utterances and then as more complicated utterances and exceptions occur, rules are added to account for these. The result is a weak analytical tool bloated by layer after layer of rules. There is no end to these potential rules and it is difficult to find any cognitive support for this view of language (i.e., a simple tool that adds layers to account for anything that does not fall within its range of analysis). Such approaches need to be abandoned as comprehensive linguistic analytical tools.

9. For more detail on this approach, see Gutt, *Translation and*

3. *Language and Society*

Many conversations in which we engage are somewhat scripted.[10] When I meet a person at an academic conference, I (or the person I meet) will probably ask something to the effect of, *What school are you at?* This question is more specific than if we met in a more neutral context such as a bus or a restaurant which might evoke a question about the weather or a local sports team. I can be more specific because I am already making assumptions about the person by his or her presence at this conference. Although the person may be a pastor or other minister, most at the conference will have a connection to a school. Also, the question, *What school are you at?*, is general enough to leave open the role the person may have at the school. He or she may be a professor or a student. If I would have asked a student *Where do you teach?*, the person may be somewhat uncomfortable because he or she may feel the need to reply, *I do not teach, I am a student*. If I would have asked a professor *Where do you study?*, the person may be offended wondering why I would have not thought he or she was a professor. Back to our original question, *What school are you at?*, is also an invitation for the person to volunteer his or her academic role of professor, student, etc., without having to be offended by my presumption of a lower role or being embarrassed by my assumption of a higher role.

Although I may be interested in the person's educational connection, if our conversation is anything like many other normal first-contact conversations, I have other reasons for asking this. I am trying to understand my social relationship to

Relevance, 24–46.

10. This section is a simple exposition of sociolinguistics. Sociolinguistics can be defined as "the study of language in relation to society" (Hudson, *Sociolinguistics*, 1 [Hudson uses italics for this statement in the original]). My purpose here is not to explore the field in any depth nor is it intended to critique or defend it. It is merely here to provide some theoretical basis for the main linguistic focus of the article. For helpful brief introductions, see Edwards, *Sociolinguistics* and Trudgill, *Sociolinguistics*. For a helpful more detailed discussion though now a little dated, see Hudson, *Sociolinguistics*.

the person. Although I (and most others) do not like to admit it, I may interact differently with a person based on how he or she responds. In the social hierarchy of academia, I will attempt to situate both of us on that hierarchy. Of course, if I have not volunteered any information, the person will then follow with a question regarding my educational role. At least from my perspective and if he or she follows social conventions, our conversation will continue as appropriate for our social roles.

A pastor mentioned to me that when meeting other pastors for the first time, he is often asked *How big is your church?* This is simple posturing for people to navigate their perceived success in relation to the other person.

Thus, language is used to help establish relationships between people.[11] In addition to what was mentioned above, we also use language to communicate information about ourselves.[12] Again, although language is obviously being used to communicate information, much more is taking place when we describe ourselves. One chooses, tweaks, and omits information in order to create a picture of oneself in accordance with how one wants to be perceived by others. In common terminology today, one desires to create a "brand" of and for him- or herself. Such image-crafting has been going on for millennia (e.g., Julius Caesar sending his commentaries on his wars to Rome). However, today dating web sites and social media take this to a whole new level. Language (and pictures, etc.) is being used to present oneself a certain way and that affects how one is perceived in relation to others.

Further, we may unintentionally communicate a number of things by our accent, writing style, etc. Our speech will often betray where we are from (dialect). The place from which we come may have positive or negative implications to others in the conversation. We are all familiar with the *shibboleth* incident in Judg 12:5–6. The Ephraimites were betrayed by their speech because they were unable to make the *sh* [š] sounds and could only say *s* [s]. While a seminary student in Dallas, my wife and I

11. Trudgill, *Sociolinguistics*, 2.
12. Trudgill, *Sociolinguistics*, 2.

were looking for apartments. In replying to an advertisement for an apartment, after hearing our voices on the phone, the apartment owner wanted to show us apartments he had not publicly listed (we did not take him up on his offer). Situations that cause less concern occur as well. When I encounter a person with a British accent, I may initiate small talk and ask him or her about what *football club* he or she supports. However, to another American, I may ask about his or her favorite *football team*. Not only is the referential sport different in the two statements, the words I use with them differ as well.

3.1 *The Influence of Language on Society and Society on Language*

Before proceeding to our Acts passage in which I hope to demonstrate the value of language's role in society, one further theoretical issue needs to be addressed. What is the relationship between society and language? In other words, does language help shape society? And/or the reverse: does society shape language?

The question of whether or not language shapes society has been ongoing.[13] Probably the most common thesis in support of the positive answer to this is the so-called "Sapir-Whorf hypothesis" named after linguists Edward Sapir and his student Benjamin Lee Whorf. Concerning this hypothesis, Peter Trudgill states,

> [S]peakers' native languages set up series of categories which act as a kind of grid through which they perceive the world, and which constrain the way in which they categorize and conceptualize different phenomena. A language can affect a society by influencing or even controlling the world-view of its speakers.[14]

In other words, language helps shape society.

13. Trudgill, *Sociolinguistics*, 1. Also, discussed as how language shapes thought (linguistic determinism), Hudson, *Sociolinguistics*, 91–105.

14. Trudgill, *Sociolinguistics*, 13. On the Sapir-Whorf hypothesis, see also Hudson, *Sociolinguistics*, 95–105.

In its extreme form, this theory has been discredited.[15] Cognitive ability and thus society is not essentially shaped by language. It is possible that in some ways available linguistic categories may influence a society resulting in somewhat unique perceptions of the world.[16] However, the fact that other societies (even those with little or no cultural connection) can generally understand these differences and translate them into their own language suggests that there is no incomprehensible uniqueness in a language.

Nevertheless, different linguistic societies may have some unique perceptions. A weak form of this theory may be acceptable if not pressed too far. Although we can often translate from language to language, there is a cost involved. The translation is often much longer and somewhat paraphrastic.[17] Further, Dirven and Verspoor discuss an experiment from child researchers in which English and Korean children classify relationships between toys differently based on either the preposition system in English (*in* and *on*) or the word *kkita* ("tight fit") in Korean. English children associated putting puzzle pieces in a puzzle with putting toys in a bag (both *in*); they also associated putting a cap on a pen with putting a hat on a doll (both *on*). However, Korean children associated putting the puzzle pieces in the puzzle with putting the cap on the pen (both *tight*); they also associated putting toys in a bag with putting a hat on a doll (both *loose*).[18] The different ways the children classified the objects suggests that their languages influenced their decisions. Thus, language has some influence on society, at least at a basic level. However, this can be overcome once one is made aware of the differences (noting the "cost" mentioned above).

15. Trudgill, *Sociolinguistics*, 15. Hudson, *Sociolinguistics*, 101. 105. One may recall that students of the Bible made judgment values about the thought potential of Jews and Greeks based on their languages. Others have seen some languages as superior to others, labelling some "primitive." For a humorous response to this approach, see Nida, *Linguistic Interludes*.

16. See the example presented by Trudgill, *Sociolinguistics*, 14–15.

17. Dirven and Verspoor, *Cognitive Exploration*, 140.

18. Dirven and Verspoor, *Cognitive Exploration*, 140–41.

An example from recent Greek studies may illustrate how languages may grammaticalize things differently than other languages resulting in somewhat different meanings and/or emphases. Until recently, English (and many other) students of the New Testament viewed the Greek verbal system essentially as a tense-oriented system. However, after further research, scholars began to see the Greek verbal system as an aspect system.[19] It is likely that the verbal systems of the non-Greek languages known by the scholars (including Latin) influenced their view of Greek. However, problems with this understanding were evident and thus led to further research resulting in the conclusion that Greek was not a tense-based but an aspect-based language. This provided a different understanding of the Greek language that was nevertheless understandable and translatable in English and other languages. Once discovered, we have been able to adjust our knowledge of the Greek verbal system to more accurately understand the meaning of the Greek text.

3.2 *The Influence of Society on Language*

Somewhat less controversial is the notion that society influences language. One need only consider words such as the verb "google" to affirm this. However, even before recent technological advances hit the mainstream, this evidence was noted. For example, where English speakers have one word for reindeer, the Sami languages of Scandinavia have several (different ages, etc.).[20] English speakers have little need for such distinction and of course it can be made if necessary (e.g., "young reindeer," etc.). Depending on the importance of people within the kinship group, some distinctions occur between languages (e.g., English uses "aunt" for both the paternal and maternal aunt; however, some languages make this specific in a single label).[21] Finally, values can affect language, especially when words are associated with what are considered taboos.[22]

19. See especially Fanning, *Verbal Aspect* and Porter, *Verbal Aspect.*
20. Trudgill, *Sociolinguistics*, 15–16.
21. Trudgill, *Sociolinguistics*, 16 (see 16–18 for this topic).
22. Trudgill, *Sociolinguistics*, 18–20.

Words that sound like taboo words are often avoided.[23] Sometimes words have changed meanings. Older terms have become associated with new things. For example, I am not comfortable reading the KJV when it refers to donkeys in the terminology of previous generations.

Much more can be said about this area. It is fascinating; however, it has less relevance for our purpose here.

4. *The Context of Acts 21:27–40*

This article has suggested that an essential component of the exegetical process is to attempt to reconstruct as much of the relevant ancient cognitive environment as possible. The more knowledge we share with the participants in the original communication situation, the more we are able to understand the intended meaning of the text. This process helps us to understand implied information that the author did not include in his original message because it was taken for granted. This aspect of the process is intended to prepare us for our main purpose. Specifically, this article explores the social use of language.

Before we turn to the social use of language in portions of Acts 21:27–40, we need to consider aspects of the context that will contribute most to highlighting the social aspect of the passage. This selective information will be useful when we turn our attention to the Acts passage. The purpose here is to lay the ground work for our Acts discussion, not engage the text at this point. Further, a full discussion of the context is beyond the scope of this work. Craig Keener's recent commentary and Ben Witherington's Socio-Rhetorical Commentary on Acts provide a wealth of contextual information, 82 and 23 pages respectively on this passage, much of which is dedicated to contextual discussion.[24] My focus will be limited to a few areas that will be essential for developing the social use of the language in the next major section.

23. For examples, see Trudgill, *Sociolinguistics*, 18–20.
24. Keener, *Acts*, 3:3113–95 and Witherington, *Acts*, 642–65.

4.1 *Immediate Literary Context*

In Acts 21:27–40, Luke records Paul's arrest in Jerusalem where he was accused of a number of things including defiling the temple. This passage is preceded by Paul's arrival and reception in Jerusalem (21:17–26). The church is excited to hear the reports about what God is doing among the Gentiles (21:19). However, it is also mentioned that many Jews have heard that Paul was instructing Jews living among Gentiles to stop obeying the Law (21:21). The church decides to take decisive action to dispel this false rumor and it is agreed that Paul will purify himself and pay expenses for others to complete their Jewish vow requirements (21:22–24). By doing this, Paul will demonstrate that these rumors are false and he himself obeys the Law (21:24). Paul then purifies himself and goes to the temple and helps the others fulfill their cultic requirements (21:26).

4.2 *Profaning the Temple*

It is no surprise that the defiling of the temple was a most serious offense to the Jews. This included non-Jews going into parts of the temple that were forbidden to Gentiles. One need only recall the atrocities of Antiochus IV in the middle of the second century BC (see 1 Macc 1:54–55; 2 Macc 6:2) and the less insidious acts of Pompey one hundred years later (see Josephus, *Ant.*, 14.71–72). Of course, this has roots in the Old Testament which provide relevant instruction and examples (Ezek 5:11; 23:38; on the tabernacle which preceded the temple, see Lev 20:3; Num 19:20). The famous temple inscription first discovered in 1871 with a second example found in 1935[25] states, "Let no foreigner enter within the screen and enclosure surrounding the sanctuary. Whosoever is taken so doing will be the cause that death overtaketh him" (OGIS 598; tr. Strachan of Deissmann[26]). Although Sherwin-White seems skeptical about the Jewish authority to put anyone to death,[27] the statement of Titus

25. Barrett, *Acts*, 2:1020. See also Josephus, *Ant.* 15.417–418 (Marcus and Wikgren, LCL) and note (d).

26. Deissmann, *Light From the Ancient East*, 80.

27. Sherwin-White, *Roman Society*, 38. He also suggests that the

recorded by Josephus is hard to dismiss, "... Was it not you that ranged along it those slabs,engraved in Greek characters and in our own, proclaiming that none can pass the barrier? And did we not permit you to put to death any who passed it? Even were he a Roman?"[28] These passages suggest that the Romans did allow the Jewish authorities to put people to death who had defiled the temple. Given the "exception-type" language of Josephus's Titus, it seem likely that this was a special circumstance.[29]

4.3 *Egyptian and an "Egyptian" in the Empire*

Egypt had been a great empire for many centuries before the New Testament period. Its large empire absorbed many peoples and with it aspects of various languages which became incorporated into Egyptian through loan words, etc.[30] However, it was the conquests of Alexander the Great and the rule of his successors in Egypt (Ptolemies) in the late fourth century which resulted in the Hellenization of Egypt.[31] Greek became the language of the Egyptian government for almost a thousand years.[32] There is evidence that the Ptolemaic rulers spoke a form of classical Greek staying close to Attic pronunciation; however, the local elites developed their own standard of pronunciation.[33]

Interestingly, the Ptolemaic and the early Roman rulers favored the Greek language over Egyptian to such an extent that

wording of the inscription is "very curious" and what is threatened here should be viewed as a "lynching" not execution.

28. Josephus, *War* 6.124–126 (Thackeray, LCL). Sherwin-White does not believe the speech itself by Titus is factual (Sherwin-White, *Roman Society*, 38). This is consistent with his position mentioned here. It is worth noting that the Flavian Dynasty was Josephus's patron family. How likely would it be to create a speech that suggests a provincial religious body had the authority to put Romans to death if not accurate?

29. See also Tajra, *Trials of St. Paul*, 123; however, Tajra cites no ancient evidence in support.

30. Ray, "Greek, Egyptian, and Coptic," 812.

31. Ray, "Greek, Egyptian, and Coptic," 812.

32. Ray, "Greek, Egyptian, and Coptic," 812.

33. Horrocks, *Greek*, 165–66. Although this is specifically about pronunciation, it follows that these speakers would have attempted to continue the Attic linguistic elements in other areas also.

"The strong position of Greek limited the written production in the Egyptian language, which already in the first century CE had virtually disappeared from the administration."[34] After almost three centuries of Ptolemaic rule, it seems Cleopatra VII was the first to actually learn Egyptian (Plutarch, *Antony* 27.4).[35] If this is accurate, the implications are significant. It is likely that there would have been a significant social distinction made between those who could speak Greek and those who could not speak Greek. Language was a means of identifying one's ethnic identity.[36] It follows that the latter group was barred from direct access to much of what Egypt could provide. They were essentially stuck in their place without very many options. Thus, language was a sign of social status. At the time of Paul, it is likely that this was a distinction of different languages. Earlier, there may have been an even more complex distinction with the Royal family and its Attic pronunciation at the top of the social hierarchy, then the rest of the Greek-speaking Egyptians, and finally those who did not speak Greek at all.

In addition, there seems to be some evidence that Romans, Greeks, and Jews all thought of Egyptians as inferior.[37] Certainly, if true, an Egyptian who only spoke an Egyptian language was susceptible to discrimination and other forms of suspicion.

Before leaving our discussion of Egypt, it is worth selectively noting one person of history that is relevant to our passage. Of course, selecting one historical element is not ideal methodologically; however, our purpose is to illuminate Acts 21:27–40 and this is sufficient for the limited purpose here.

34. Torallas Tovar, "Greek in Egypt," 256.

35. Torallas Tovar, "Greek in Egypt," 256; Thompson, "Cleopatra VII," 333.

36. Torallas Tovar, "Greek in Egypt," 256. It is likely that Greek with a strong local accent would also be seen negatively. However, for the purpose of this article, I will focus on the significant difference between languages and not on dialects of the same language. Concerning the Acts passage, I will suggest the distinction of languages is the issue (see below).

37. See Keener, *Acts,* 3:3178–80, and the literature cited there.

During the governorship of Felix (AD 52–59),[38] an Egyptian false-prophet arose and caused significant trouble in Judea. Josephus states,

> At this time there came to Jerusalem from Egypt a man who declared that he was a prophet and advised the masses of the common people to go out with him to the mountain called the Mount of Olives, which lies opposite the city at a distance of five furlongs. For he asserted that he wished to demonstrate from there that at his command Jerusalem's walls would fall down, through which he promised to provide them an entrance into the city. When Felix heard of this he ordered his soldiers to take up their arms. Setting out from Jerusalem with a large force of cavalry and infantry, he fell upon the Egyptian and his followers, slaying four hundred of them and taking two hundred prisoners. The Egyptian himself escaped from the battle and disappeared.[39]

In this passage and the parallel in *Jewish War*, Josephus notes that the Egyptian escaped. The *Antiquities* passage here states that he "escaped (διαδράς) and disappeared (ἀφανὴς ἐγένετο)," leaving no finality to the potential trouble he may still cause (at least for the people who lived at the time of the recorded event). Thus, during the time of Paul there was a man at large whose actions resulted in horrible damage to many lives, and probably more importantly, disrupted the Roman peace. Such an individual would have caused the empire to be on alert.[40]

38. The termination of Felix's governorship is disputed. Here I follow Bruce who bases this date on coinage (*New Testament History*, 345–46).

39. Josephus, *Ant.*, 20.169–172 (Feldman, LCL). See also Josephus, *War* 2.261–263. For a brief discussion of both passages, see Schürer, *History of the Jewish People*, 464.

40. A further helpful contextual issue for understanding the Acts passage would be to explore the relationship between local city-citizenship and Roman citizenship. However, this is less significant for the particular focus of this paper. For helpful information on this, see Keener, *Acts*, 3:3178–87; Rapske, *Paul in Roman Custody*, 141–42; and Tajra, *Trial of St. Paul*, 76–80.

5. *Acts 21:27–40 and the Social Use of Language*

I am now prepared to discuss the social use of language in Acts 21:27–40. Since speech seems to be most naturally used for social purposes, this is what will be examined. Three speech incidents occur in this passage: verses 28, 36, and 37–39. I will only discuss the first and the last.

Some may correctly note that these speech contributions are delivered through the pen of the author of Acts, Luke. We do not have direct access to the original statements. This is not the place for debating the accuracy of reported speeches in Luke's writings. Whether or not this reflects historical reality has no impact on my conclusion. The effect of the statements on the narrative is the same.

5.1 *The Accusation: 21:28*

Paul is seen in the temple and because he is seen earlier with Trophimus, a Gentile from Ephesus (Acts 21:29), an accusation is made by Jews from Asia against him (Acts 21:28):

> People of Israel, help! This is the man who is teaching everyone everywhere against our people, our Law, and this place; in addition also, he has brought Greeks into the temple and has defiled this holy place.[41]

A number of charges are brought against Paul. It is uncertain whether the accusers actually believed all their charges or were exaggerating (they certainly used hyperbole in their accusation, "teaching everyone everywhere"). Nevertheless, these Jews probably had previous experience with Paul in Asia and saw him as a threat to them and/or Judaism. Luke's narrative makes it clear that the charges are baseless. Nevertheless, the intended audience, the Jews in Jerusalem, believed them, banded together, and rushed the temple, seized Paul and tried to kill him (21:30–31). The Roman tribune and his soldiers intervened and rescued Paul.

The charges against Paul for his teaching may be based on a misunderstanding of Paul's words. Certainly, neither in Acts nor

41. All New Testament translations are my own.

in his letters does Paul teach against the Jews, their Law, or the temple. Nevertheless, based on his views and his Gentile mission, it is understandable that he could be perceived this way by some.[42] This is unfortunate because Paul's presence in the temple was intended to demonstrate the opposite.

It is probably no accident that the final charge, defiling the temple, is included and emphasized (a further clause is used to develop the charge against the temple) even if only based on speculation. It is this charge that holds the most serious consequences. This seems to be the only charge that could result in capital punishment. Thus, the statement made by the Asian Jews is much more than a list of charges. It is a call to the Jews to rise up and kill Paul.[43] The arrival of the Romans is in response to the unrest. There is no indication that they understood what the commotion was about. They save Paul; however, this does not mean they would not have allowed Paul to be killed if the charge of temple defilement was proven.

Thus, the Asian Jews understood their Jerusalem context well. They chose their words to accomplish their goal. The charge of defiling the temple was essentially an order to kill Paul.

5.2 *The Egyptian*

Through recent events and possibly through some information from the crowd (21:33), the Roman tribune apparently believed he had in his custody the Egyptian false prophet that had caused so much trouble in the past. I realize there is significant debate on whether the tribune associated Paul with the Egyptian prior to or only after Paul spoke. I am assuming the former but with acknowledgment that this conclusion is not without problems.[44]

42. See Keener's discussion of Paul's Temple theology (*Acts,* 3:3150–52).

43. See the discussion above in 4.2. Also, Rowe, *World Upside Down*, 63 and 212, nn. 54 and 55.

44. The use of the negative οὐκ in a Greek questions usually assumes a positive answer (BDF §440; for οὐκ with ἄρα as here, BDF suggests "astonishment"; §440[2]).This would seem to suggest that it is Paul's use of Greek that leads the tribune to make the identification. Although with some differences and not all explicitly using Greek grammar for their conclusion, see

Also, if the latter is concluded, those aspects of my analysis that are not dependent upon the specific identification of Paul as the Egyptian false prophet are still valid (my purpose is to demonstrate the social use of language). If the tribune believed Paul to be the Egyptian, this is one reason the tribune may have wished to intervene. This man should face Roman justice.

However, the tribune is surprised when Paul speaks. Luke records the conversation as follows (Acts 21:37–39):

> While Paul was about to be brought into the soldier's camp, he said to the tribune, "is it permitted that I say something to you?" And he [the tribune] replied, "Do you know Greek? Then you are not the Egyptian who in the past started a revolt and led four thousand assassins out into the desert?" And Paul replied, "I am a Jewish man from Tarsus in Cilicia, a citizen of an important city; I ask you, allow me speak to the people."

As noted above, there are a number of fruitful areas of inquiry related to the social use of language in this passage (e.g., Paul's claim of have citizenship with the city of Tarsus). However, I will limit my discussion to the mis-identification of Paul as the Egyptian false prophet.

The tribune assumes he has the Egyptian false prophet in custody. The scale of the disturbance due to Paul's presence may have led to this misunderstanding. In light of the notorious nature of this individual, the modern reader may wonder why he was mis-identified. However, we must remember that the absence of photographs, etc., made it difficult to identify people without whom one did not have personal experience. It is the actions and response of the crowd that led to this identification, not Paul's physical characteristics.

This response suggests that the Roman believed that this Egyptian false prophet was of low birth and status. This may be

Bock, *Acts*, 657; Witherington, *Acts*, 661. However, it seems preferable to see that it is Paul's use of the Greek language that causes the tribune to question his original conclusion that this was the Egyptian (see Bruce, *Acts*, 412; Conzelmann, *Acts*, 183; Pervo, *Acts*, 553). One cannot make too much of the intended expectation for the answer to the question with οὐκ. Rather, as Pervo suggests, "Interpretation must be based on the narrative, rather than on historical or linguistic argument" (*Acts,* 553, n. 32).

true. He apparently did not speak (or was thought to have not spoken) Greek.[45] It appears that the Romans did not even attempt to talk with him. They were probably on their way to interrogate Paul when he spoke. The assumed language difference and the contempt that they had for the Egyptian made communication unlikely. However, once Paul asks his question, the entire situation changes. The change is not the result of the content of the words Paul spoke. He did not persuade the tribune of anything with his propositional information. It was simply Paul's ability to speak Greek that impacted the situation.

Thus, with Paul's simple statement, everything changed. He no longer was seen as the infamous criminal. Nor was he viewed as a lowly Egyptian. Instead, Paul's use of Greek elevated him in the eyes of the tribune. It is possible that Paul's claim of citizenship in Tarsus was intended to build upon the tribune's question. This association would possibly make Paul's Greek even more impressive.[46]

Here then is another example of language making an impact on an event beyond the content of the statement itself. The use of Greek by Paul has given him a higher standing in the Roman tribune's eyes. It is likely that this change in perception resulted

45. It is possible that it is Paul's "high" dialect or accent of Greek expressed in his question recorded in v. 37 (εἰ ἔξεστίν μοι εἰπεῖν τι πρὸς σέ;) that gets the tribune's attention ("the quality of Paul's Greek" [Pervo, *Acts*, 553]; see also Keener, *Acts,* 3:3168–72). However, without strong evidence to the contrary (I do not believe that the wording of the question is strong evidence), it seems that this is a language not a dialect or accent issue. How can one make dialect conclusions with such a small sample and how can one know accent without oral communication or statements making this explicit? Nevertheless, the social implications would be the same. Conclusions here based on the difference in language can be applied to differences in dialect and accent. Dialects and accents viewed as inferior would have social consequences.

46. Returning to the option not concluded above that the tribune did not associate Paul with the Egyptian until after he spoke, the social use of language is still evident. In this case, Paul was assumed to be a lowly troublemaker. His use of Greek would result in the tribune assuming that he was the Egyptian. Thus, Paul's explanation is intended to dispel this association.

in the tribune allowing Paul to address the Jewish people and to avoid interrogation (at least for the time being).

6. *Conclusion*

This brief article has attempted to demonstrate that in addition to carrying content in a communication situation, language can also be used in a social manner. This "meaning" is not part of the "linguistic meaning" of the text. This was demonstrated in Acts 21:27–40 in two ways. First, Paul is charged with violating the temple. This offense, if proven, will result in the death of the offender. It is likely that Paul's accusers knew this and this is why the charge is included and highlighted in their accusation. Second, Paul's use of Greek elevates his status in the opinion of a Roman tribune. This results in Paul avoiding interrogation for the time being and being given permission to address the crowd.

The social use of language cannot be ignored. Acknowledgment of this use of language and active incorporation of this information will result in more complete exegetical results.

Bibliography

Barrett, C.K. *The Acts of the Apostles*. 2 vols. ICC. Edinburgh: T. & T. Clark, 1994–1998.

Blakemore, Diane. *Relevance and Linguistic Meaning: The Semantics and Pragmatics of Discourse Markers.* Cambridge Studies in Linguistics 99. Cambridge: Cambridge University Press, 2002.

Bock, Darrell L. *Acts*. BECNT. Grand Rapids: Baker, 2007.

Bruce, F.F. *New Testament History*. Garden City, NY: Doubleday, 1980.

_______. *The Book of Acts*. NICNT. Grand Rapids: Eerdmans, 1988.

Conzelmann, Hans. *Acts of the Apostles: A Commentary on the Acts of the Apostles*. Translated by James Limburg and A. Thomas Kraabel. Hermeneia. Philadelphia: Fortress Press, 1987.

Deissmann, Adolf. *Light from the Ancient East: The New Testament Illustrated by Recently Discovered Texts of the Graeco-Roman World.* Translated by Lionel R. Strachan. Reprinted, Peabody, MA: Hendrickson, 1995.

Dirven, René, and Marjolijn Verspoor. *Cognitive Exploration of Language and Linguistics*. Cognitive Linguistics in Practice. Amsterdam: John Benjamins, 1998.

Edwards, John. *Sociolinguistics: A Very Short Introduction.* Oxford: Oxford University Press, 2013.

Engberg-Pedersen, Troels. "Introduction." In *Paul Beyond the Judaism/Hellenism Divide*, 1–16. Louisville, KY: Westminster John Knox Press, 2001.

Fanning, Buist M. *Verbal Aspect in New Testament Greek.* Oxford Theological Monographs. Oxford: Clarendon, 1990.

Fantin, Joseph D. "Background Studies: Grounding the Text in Reality." In *Interpreting the New Testament Text: Introduction to the Art and Science of Exegesis*, edited by Darrell L. Bock and Buist M. Fanning, 167–96. Wheaton, IL: Crossway, 2006.

_______. *The Greek Imperative Mood in the New Testament: A Cognitive and Communicative Approach.* Studies in Biblical Greek 12. New York: Peter Lang, 2010.

_______. *The Lord of the Entire Word: Lord Jesus, a Challenge to Lord Caesar?* New Testament Monographs 31. Sheffield: Sheffield Phoenix Press, 2011.

Grice, H. Paul. "Logic and Conversation." In *Syntax and Semantics, Vol. 3: Speech Acts*, edited by P. Cole and J. Morgan, 41–58. New York: Academic Press, 1975.

_______. "Further Notes on Logic and Conversation." In *Syntax and Semantics, Vol. 9: Pragmatics*, edited by P. Cole, 113–27. New York: Academic Press, 1978.

Gutt, Ernst-August. *Translation and Relevance: Cognition and Context.* 2nd ed. Manchester: St. Jerome, 2000.

Horrocks, Geoffrey C. *Greek: A History of the Language and Its Speakers*. 2nd ed. Chichester, UK: Wiley-Blackwell, 2010.

Hudson, R.A. *Sociolinguistics*. 2nd ed. Cambridge Textbooks in Linguistics. Cambridge: Cambridge University Press, 1996.

Keener, Craig S. *Acts: An Exegetical Commentary.* 3 vols. to date. Grand Rapids: Baker, 2012–2014.

Nida, Eugene. *Linguistic Interludes*. Santa Ana, CA: Summer Institute of Linguistics, 1947.

Pervo, Richard I. *Acts: A Commentary*. Hermeneia. Philadelphia: Fortress Press, 2009.

Porter, Stanley E. *Verbal Aspect in the Greek of the New Testament with Reference to Tense and Mood.* 2nd ed. Studies in Biblical Greek 1. New York: Peter Lang, 1993.

Rapske, Brian. *Paul in Roman Custody*. The Book of Acts in its First Century Setting, vol. 3. Grand Rapids: Eerdmans, 1994.

Ray, J. "Greek, Egyptian, and Coptic." In *A History of Ancient Greek: From Beginnings to Late Antiquity*, edited by Anastossios-Fivos Christidis, 811–18. Cambridge: Cambridge University Press, 2007.

Rowe, C. Kavin. *World Upside Down: Reading Acts in the Graeco-Roman Age*. Oxford: Oxford University Press, 2009.

Schürer, Emil. *The History of the Jewish People in the Age of Jesus Christ (175 B.C.–A.D. 135)*. Revised and edited by Geza Vermes et al. Edinburgh: T. & T. Clark, 1973.

Sperber, Dan, and Deirdre Wilson. *Relevance: Communication and Cognition*. 2nd ed. Oxford: Blackwell, 1995.

Tajra, Harry W. *The Trials of St. Paul: A Juridical Exegesis of the Second Half of the Acts of the Apostles*. WUNT 2.35. Tübingen: Mohr Siebeck, 1989.

Thompson, Dorothy J. "Cleopatra VII." In *The Oxford Classical Dictionary*, edited by Simon Hornblower et al., 333. 4th ed. Oxford: Oxford University Press, 2012.

Torallas Tovar, Sofia. "Greek in Egypt." In *A Companion to the Ancient Greek Language*, edited by Egbert J. Bakker, 253–66. Blackwell Companions to the Ancient World. Chichester, UK: Wiley-Blackwell, 2010.

Trudgill, Peter. *Sociolinguistics: An Introduction to Language and Society*. 4th ed. London: Penguin, 2000.

Sherwin-White, A.N. *Roman Society and Roman Law in the New Testament: The Sarum Lectures 1960–1961*. Oxford: Clarendon, 1963.

Witherington, Ben, III. *The Acts of the Apostles: A Socio-Rhetorical Commentary*. Grand Rapids: Eerdmans, 1998.

[*BAGL* 4 (2015) 30–48]

The Living Language Environment of Acts 21:27–40

Jonathan M. Watt
Geneva College, Beaver Falls, PA, USA

Abstract: A sociolinguistic approach to Paul's language usage in the Jerusalem arrest narratives of Acts 21–22 offers inferences with regard to his specific language choices between Greek, Hebrew and Aramaic during his interactions. However, modern language studies show considerable inter-language penetration that, by implication, complicates conclusions one may reach with regard to the New Testament situation. (Article)

Keywords: sociolinguistics, multilingualism, linguistic repertoire, code-switching, cross-linguistic penetration.

1. *Introduction*

In a discussion of rhetorical constructions such as elliptical zeugma and brachylogy in his epic 1934 grammar, A.T. Robertson references an instance of *hypallage* (an unexpected interchange of word segments) in the Fourth Gospel involving the adjectival/attribut*ed* genitive phrase often translated "full of grace."[1] Responding critically to discussions of how the ancient writer 'should' have worded something, Robertson admits that the apostolic author "used repetition of word and phrase" in atypical fashion but crisply affirms that "[t]he papyri have taught

1. Robertson, *Grammar*, 1204. See also Wallace, *Greek Grammar*, 89–91. This paper was originally presented at the New Testament Greek Language and Exegesis consultation of the Annual Meeting of the Evangelical Theological Society, San Diego, CA, November 19, 2014.

us to be chary about charging John with being ungrammatical in πλήρης χάριτος (John 1:14). These matters simply show that the N.T. writers used a live language and were not automata."[2] In short, Robertson affirmed that a fluent speaker's language *performance* may contravene the expectation of a theoretical grammarian who lives apart from the original living language environment. As in the case of the gospel's writer, a competent speaker with firsthand experience of his own linguistic environment may defy scholarly expectation even as he writes (as Robertson put it) "with consummate skill and marvelous vividness and dramatic power."[3]

Sociolinguists are avid observers of that "consummate skill," being as one seasoned practitioner, Alan Bell, has put it, "professional eavesdroppers—not on what people say, but on how they are saying it."[4] Citing Dell Hymes, Bell notes that sociolinguists are on the hunt for three things: social issues which have a language component, "real-society data," and evidence which shows that "language is inherently social and society is inherently linguistic."[5] In other words, these eavesdroppers are simultaneously theoretical-deductive as well as observational-inductive, both idealists and pragmatists. Whether one eats one's Reese's Peanut Butter Cup outward from the soft center, or inward from its crenellated periphery, sociolinguistics has something to offer everyone.

Language and culture engage in mutual dialogue: on the one hand, context shapes how language is used and, on the other, speakers address culture and instruct it on how it 'should' be done. Multilinguals make language choices based on factors rooted simultaneously in the external circumstances fixed around them and in perceptions rooted deep in their own minds which often (though not always) align with their surroundings. Ronald Wardhaugh suggests:

2. Robertson, *Grammar*, 1204.
3. Robertson, *Grammar*, 1204.
4. Bell, *Guidebook to Sociolinguistics*, 1.
5. Bell, *Guidebook to Sociolinguistics*, 2.

> There are several possible relationships between language and society. One is that social structure may either influence or determine linguistic structure and/or behavior . . . [and] a second possible relationship is directly opposed to the first: linguistic structure and/or behavior may either influence or determine social structure. This is the view that is behind the [Sapir-]Whorfian hypothesis . . . . A third possible relationship is that the influence is bi-directional: language and society may influence each other.[6]

This paper follows that bi-directional frame, being oriented toward Wardhaugh's suggestion that there is a helpful distinction to be made between *sociolinguistics as micro-linguistics* or the study of language in relation to society, and *sociology of language as macro-linguistics* or the study of society in relation to language.[7] The former examines language and society with a view to understanding the nature of language while the latter inverts the order. Wardhaugh adds that the former (i.e. socio- or micro-linguistics) looks at how social structures (e.g. class, age, gender) influence the ways people talk, while the latter (sociology/macro-linguistics) considers what societies do with their languages, including attitudes toward language, functional distribution of varieties, language shift and maintenance, and so forth.[8] We can straddle that fence, paying attention to the *collective repertoire of a community* (what society says to the speaker) and also to the *repertoire of individual speakers* (which may be broader or narrower than the community's; this is what the speaker believes is most appropriate)—and to the ideologies of language that arise from either side of that equation.

One caveat that should be mentioned here relates to the dissonance between the title of this paper and the nature of the evidence that must be cited in all the literature on this subject: that which is "living" versus that which is inscribed. A written source's language is not necessarily equivalent to the original living language of a reported event. Baltes appropriately notes, for example, that an ossuary inscription could reflect the

6. Wardhaugh, *Introduction to Sociolinguistics*, 10.

7. Wardhaugh, *Introduction to Sociolinguistics*, 12–13; Hudson, *Sociolinguistics*, 4.

8. Wardhaugh, *Introduction to Sociolinguistics*, 2.

language of the person who is buried, of the one who commissioned the inscription, of the ossuary decorator, or of the intended reader of the inscription; or "it could simply be the language perceived to be culturally appropriate for the occasion."[9] This adds a layer of complexity that necessarily haunts this area of investigation. Nevertheless, we must press on in the spirit of Robertson's contention that a fluent speaker possesses "skill and vividness" in wielding his repertoire, and will engage the way sociolinguists capture the situation by applying concepts of the field to Acts 21:27–40. We shall ask certain questions about how a multicultural Jewish-Christian leader, being detained in a Roman stronghold adjacent to an historic center of Jewish worship, chose to speak—for by all accounts, this situation presents a curious set of discordant cultural factors that are sure to yield some interesting results.

2. *What is the Language Situation behind Acts 21?*

Although this is the necessary and natural beginning point, I will devote the least amount of attention to it because much has been written on the subject, and previous conferences and publications have given considerable attention to the usage of Hebrew (Biblical and Mishnaic), Aramaic, Greek and (to a limited degree) Latin. More useful right now will be the concept of *repertoire*, that collection of codes from which multilingual speakers select their mode of communication. In its simplest formulation, the factors of social circumstances act as *independent variables*, the givens of each situation, which exert an influence on the choices one makes from codes available in that repertoire which comprise a set of dependent variables that become activated in response to the needs of each social setting.

The community's repertoire is often subject to a *functional distribution*, especially when it experiences a particular form of bilingualism known as *diglossia*.[10] With *diglossia*, particular

9. Baltes, "Use of Hebrew and Aramaic," 53–54.

10. Watt, "Bilingualism"; Buth and Notley, *Language Environment*; and

assignments ('high' and 'low') are to be given to each type of code, and each is expected to be used in a particular situation (parallel to general bilingualism, in which case the codes are different languages; e.g. English is *the* language of international aviation regardless of the plane's location or the pilot's native language). Significant features of social setting include what is formal/informal and public/private, the topic and purpose of the conversation, the relationship of the speakers to each other, whether the context is religious or civil, and so forth—though the lines of demarcation defining these features are uniquely delineated by different communities. The *functional distribution* of the codes in a first-century Palestinian Jewish repertoire, for example, *could* prompt Jesus to select Aramaic in the presence of a bereft Galilean family (Mark 5:41) as the colloquial code for close social proximity; Hebrew, when in discussion with temple teachers (Luke 2:46–47) since it was the language of the sacred Scriptures and suitable for rabbinic instruction; and Greek with Pontius Pilate (John 18:28–38) since it was the *lingua franca* of the Mediterranean world at that time. That the *titulus* posted on the cross was inscribed also in Latin (John 19:19–20) implies both the authority behind the formal condemnation and perhaps a presumption of selective comprehension within the occupied community.

However, it must be noted that multilingual societies are notorious for having considerable differences between their speakers' individual repertoires, and also for having widely diverse competency levels between personal repertoires.[11] This ragged picture means that sociolinguistics properly starts by framing the big picture of what speech habits generally occur in bilingual communities, and this brief introduction to related issues is intended only as an orientation to these foundational considerations of multilingual repertoires, (in-)dependent variables, *diglossia* and functional distribution. The literature is extensive and readily available.

Ong, "Linguistics Analysis."

11. Watt, "Bilingualism."

3. *What is the Domain in Acts 21:27–40?*

Subsequent to the conclusion of the cross-continental itineration of Paul's third missionary journey, the apostle and his companions arrive in Jerusalem (Acts 21:17) presumably with the intention of circulating back up to Syrian Antioch. While in Jerusalem, Paul meets with fellow believers and then ascends the temple mount, likely after making use of one of the *mikvoth* (21:26) positioned adjacent to it. He is careful not to take Greek visitors beyond the *soreq* (21:29) but is suspected of doing so anyway, and consequently he is mobbed by a zealous crowd that has been agitated by Jews visiting Jerusalem from Asia Minor (21:27, 30). Alerted to the commotion, the Roman chiliarch who is stationed at the adjacent Antonia fortress takes Paul into protective custody (21:31–36), but as he hurries his prisoner toward the fortress—a trip of no more than a few hundred yards—he is addressed by his captive in Greek (21:37–39), a surprise that buys Paul enough time to clarify that he is hardly an insurrectionist but a Jew of reputable standing *and* a Roman citizen (21:39). The speech that follows these events (22:1–21) was given τῇ Ἑβραΐδι διαλέκτῳ (21:40; also 22:2)—to which I will return—a move which garners respectful silence momentarily, at least until he goes on to mention evangelism to Gentiles.[12]

This contextual view will help identify some important circumstances relating to the domain of 21:27–40. *Domain* is "an abstraction which refers to a sphere of activity representing a combination of specific times, settings and role relationships."[13] It may be predicated on things like family, friendship, religion or education, and it provides "anchor points for distinct value systems" that tend to lead people toward specified language usage. The domain of the temple mount and its Jewish activities might call for Aramaic as the vernacular of Palestinian Jewry, but also Hebrew, as has been attested elsewhere as the language of

12. For recent discussion, see Buth and Pierce, "*Hebraisti*," especially 97, for its relevance to Acts 21–22.

13. Romaine, *Language in Society*, 44.

temple police commands, not to mention the more obvious language of the Jewish Scriptures (ANT 5:272).[14] Greek was not prohibited, but would surely be dispreferred by some people in that setting. It is illuminating to consider the three dozen documents discovered by Yigael Yadin from the "Cave of Letters" with its various materials from AD 73–132; most are in Greek, though some are written in Aramaic and Hebrew, and six are in Nabataean. One item is a letter to Bar Kochba that apologizes for writing in Greek instead of Hebrew.[15] There are indicators of intentionality, even formality, on Paul's part, including the fact that he stood, motioned with his hands, and then proceeded to speak (Acts 21:40), addressing them as "brothers and fathers." Together these motions elicited "a great hush" (NASB) that became even more so once his Ἑβραΐδι was heard by them (22:2). One wonders whether his register or some specific word choices in his address might have affirmed his personal identification with Jerusalem (22:3). The depicting of the occasion urges consideration of Hebrew as the medium of address.

Also relevant to the discussion is Paul's prior and explicitly identified use of Greek (Acts 21:37) when speaking to the Roman chiliarch. It has been shown elsewhere in the literature that, by the latter years of the Republic, Rome had drawn Hellenistic Greek westward as a language of advanced literacy and wider communication.[16] The striking thing about Paul's language choice in Acts 21:37 was not the Greek but the location, for in those circumstances the chiliarch expected *something* Semitic. Studies of language ideology indicate that values related to religion, nationality, and kinship exert considerable pressure upon one's code of preference for a given situation. Curiously, as Safrai notes in connection with use of Hebrew amongst the Galilean population, educational level is not necessarily in direct proportion to multilingualism, as shown

14. Buth and Kvasnica, "Temple Authorities."

15. See Eshel, "Use of Hebrew Language," 251–52; also Baltes, "Use of Hebrew and Aramaic," 61–62.

16. Watt, "Brief History."

by numerous modern parallels; people acquire auxiliary languages either by formal study or informal use (or both), and the value of living usage exceeds the potentials of "book work."[17] The diversity of occasions for the use of Hebrew (as shown in Safrai, for example)—temple, synagogue Torah readings, instruction/discussion, and prayer, not to mention formal documents (also Eshel)—in other words, the *breadth of functional distribution*, helps strengthen the case for a wider Hebrew competence that has sometimes been allowed by modern scholars.

4. *In What Language Did Paul Speak To The Crowd?*

The Aramaic versus Hebrew discussion over the past century has seen deviations in course. The traditionally Hebrew-centered picture was supplanted by an "Exclusive Aramaic Model" on an assumption of the morbidity of living (i.e. spoken) Hebrew.[18] The Aramaic model then went through a refinement pertaining to which dialect (and period) of Aramaic was at issue, and a gradual consideration of developments in twentieth-century linguistics that shed light on the issue. Part of the picture that brings in a living/spoken Hebrew (Mishnaic) is the growing evidence that the functional distribution of Hebrew and Aramaic did not involve such mutually exclusive assignments as was once thought to exist: "[T]he assumption that Hebrew was exclusively used for religious purposes while Aramaic was used for all other matters, cannot be verified from the epigraphic sources," concludes Baltes.[19] Additionally, the assumption that Hebrew was for the learned and Aramaic the general uneducated population is increasingly unsustainable. This picture is painted similarly by Millard, whose survey of everyday writings (from kitchenware to construction beams) led him to conclude that "The surviving examples of writing from Herodian Palestine and

17. Safrai, "Spoken and Literary Languages," 231–32.
18. See description in Baltes, "Origins," 9–34, of its development.
19. Baltes, "Use of Hebrew and Aramaic," 64.

the available literary references show that writing in Greek, Aramaic and Hebrew was widespread and could be found at all levels of society."[20] The *titulus* on the cross is a much-discussed example of this, and it shows what would be expected if, as Baltes concludes,

> From the statistical overview of language use the clear picture emerges of a trilingual society in which Greek, Aramaic and Hebrew are used side by side and even in close interaction with each other. None of the three languages can be said to be dominant. Generally speaking, there is a prevalence of the Semitic languages over Greek (at least in the New Testament era) and, within the Semitic languages, a prevalence of Aramaic over Hebrew, however not to a significant degree.[21]

The same can be said for Jesus' cry from the cross, "My God, My God, why have you forsaken me?" Two gospels report this quotation but differ in their wording: Matt 27:46 reports *ηλι, ηλι, λεμα σαβαχθανι*, while Mark 15:34 has *ελωι*.[22] The verb appears to be Aramaized Hebrew, transliterated of course into Greek. Other parts of the New Testament specifically tag and translate such code-switches (e.g. John 5:2; 19:13, 17, 20; 20:16; Acts 21:40; Rev 9:11; 16:16) but these may leave unanswered exactly which language is being tagged. Joseph Fitzmyer notes that:

> Greek writers of a later period refer to the language [Aramaic] as συριστί or συριακή. When, however, Greek writers of the first century refer to the native Semitic language of Palestine, they use ἑβραϊστί, ἑβραΐς, διάλεκτος, or ἑβραΐζων. As far as I can see, no one has yet found the adverb *aramaïsti*. The adverb ἑβραϊστί (and its related expressions) seem to mean "in Hebrew," and it has often been argued that it means this and nothing more. As is well known, it is used at times with words and expressions that are clearly Aramaic. Thus in John 19:13, ἑβραϊστὶ δὲ Γαββαθᾶ is given as an explanation of the Lithostrotos, and γαββαθᾶ is a Grecized form of the Aramaic word *gabbĕtâ*, "raised place." This long-standing, thorny question is

20. Millard, *Reading and Writing*, 210.

21. Baltes, "Use of Hebrew and Aramaic," 53. See also the discussion in 47–52.

22. See Buth, "The Riddle of Jesus' Cry," for extensive discussion.

still debated; and unfortunately, the Greek letter of Bar Cochba (?) cited earlier does not shed a ray of light on the meaning of ἑβραϊστί.[23]

In response, Buth and Pierce argue that *Hebraisti* always points to Hebrew and never to Aramaic "in attested texts during the Second Temple and Greco-Roman periods."[24] Furthermore, Buth and Kvasnica argue that "it is imperative that Hebrew be restored to an active diagnostic role"[25]—though in a subsequent volume in that 2014 series edited by Buth and Notley, Ruzer suggests that some ancient sources, including Hellenistic Jewish ones, did not always "distinguish between the two closely related languages," and Philo's own writings are "a witness for . . . the possibility that Aramaic and Hebrew would remain undifferentiated in Diaspora Jewish perception . . . ."[26] However, none of these implies that the difference was always left unclarified. It is noteworthy that Acts 6:1 presents a dichotomy between the complaints τῶν Ἑλληνιστῶν and τοὺς Ἑβραίους. Commentaries differ on whether they understand these as ethno-cultural or linguistic identifiers, but in either case it leaves open the likelihood that some ancient writers were less concerned with language nomenclature (of course ancient Jewish authors could distinguish one language from the other) and more focused on what distinguished one ethnic group (e.g. Jews) from others.

Along these same lines, Kuhn suggests that the use of Ἑβραῖος in Greek inscriptions was sometimes preferred over Ἰουδαῖος because the latter term could be perceived as "derogatory and contemptuous" while the former was "lofty."[27] He proposes that the word conveyed the "national characteristics of Palestinian Jews . . . who maintained their Palestinian traits, primarily of using Aramaic as their mother tongue, in distinction from Jews of the *diaspora* who had fully adapted themselves to the surrounding world in language and manner of life."[28] In Acts

23. Fitzmyer, *Semitic Background*, 43. Question mark his.
24. Buth and Pierce, "*Hebraisti*," 109.
25. Buth and Kvasnica, "Temple Authorities," 77.
26. Ruzer, "Hebrew versus Aramaic as Jesus' Language," 184–85.
27. Kuhn, "Jewish Literature," 368–69.
28. Kuhn, "Jewish Literature," 368.

21:40 and 22:2, the word strongly suggests Hebrew or something Hebraic (see below for what is implied here), intended more as a reference to the language habits of a people group—in contrast to outsiders, Paul was an insider—for what was being identified was *the speech of Palestinian Jews*. In principle, Hebrew seems to be the most compelling choice here, as it presses the fact of Paul's expertise on matters pertinent to the domain in which that language would be most compelling.

5. *What do Modern (Living) Language Parallels Offer?*

It might appear that Hebrew 'wins' over Aramaic, both on epigraphic and sociolinguistic (including domain-related) grounds. However, when it comes to the matter of discourse there is a necessary qualification. The classic formulations of traditional sociolinguistics relating independent (sociological) to dependent (linguistic) variables is undergoing scrutiny even when it comes to basic concepts such as language and dialect choices. "Language cannot be tamed to an idealized standard. It is always and everywhere variegated,"[29] says Bell (also quoting Bakhtin) and adding that: "At any given moment of its historical existence, language is heteroglot from top to bottom: it represents the co-existence of socio-ideological contradictions between the present and the past, between different epochs of the past, between different socio-ideological groups in the present, between tendencies, schools, circles and so forth, all given a bodily form."[30] One begins to suspect that even late Second Temple Judaism might also have experienced a hyphenated history (with apologies to Gottwald and Mendenhall).

This spirit of hyphenation (and Bakhtin) lurks behind Braj Kachru's depiction of the relationship of language to culture: he sees concentric circles in which language is the site of a struggle between peripheralizing centrifugal forces which pull it toward diversity and centripetal forces that promote standardization and

29. Bell, *Guidebook to Sociolinguistics*, 3.
30. Bakhtin, "Discourse," 291.

prescription. Illustrating via English, Kachru observes that first-language nations such as England and the United States provide a putative norm for language while second-language English-speaking nations such as Malaysia and India constitute an outer circle which promotes variations on the norms; the expanding circle of ESL nations (such as Korea and Germany) is expected in turn to adapt to the norms.[31] Canagarajah's adaptation of Kachru's framework holds that English is being simultaneously vernacularized and pluralized.[32] If one turns to Greek and Palestinian Aramaic, a parallel suggests itself: the former is being internationalized and peripheralized because of its second language role across the Mediterranean, while the latter is caught in a toss-up between Classical/literary Hebrew (standardization) and the local vernacularizing needs which find Aramaic convenient while holding the original language of the Scriptures in high regard. The outcomes of these centripetal and centrifugal forces would then apply to Mishnaic Hebrew and Semiticized Greek, as both become subject to the tension between what had occurred historically on a literary level and that which was occurring in an oral environment. In multilingual (and specifically *diglossic*) societies, speakers differ in their idiosyncratic usage and, accordingly, diversity can be expected amongst first-century Palestinian Jews as well. As Safrai notes, the diversity of language choice he cites with regard to legal documents "reflects a consequence of the spiritual quandary and national crisis" of the latter part of that century, adding that "Either Hebrew or Aramaic was used in the synagogue or at other communal gatherings, but there are a number of questions concerning the relationship of these two languages in the land of Israel."[33]

So a different sort of question is in order, given that Acts 21 depicts oral discourse: rather than ask 'What Language?' one perhaps ought to ask 'How?' instead. Paul would 'need' to use

31. Kachru, "Teaching World Englishes."

32. Canagarajah, *Resisting Linguistic Imperialism*; see also discussion in Bell, *Guidebook to Sociolinguistics*, 278–80.

33. Safrai, "Spoken and Literary Languages," 258.

something Semitic in the temple setting and would have to balance the needs of those people who expected Hebrew along with all whose competence was stronger in Aramaic. After all, he was facing a multitude (some translations have 'crowd' or 'rabble' Acts 21:27, 30, 34, 35, 36) and that implies diversity, including diversity of competence. Their situation would be similar to that of the Old Order Amish of North America today: German is the traditional and expected language of Bible reading in worship services, but there is a limited understanding of Modern High German, especially among younger attendants; Pennsylvania German vernacular is the most readily understood. In such *diglossic* arrangements, inter-language penetration is especially common, as evidenced as well in Jesus' words from the cross (mentioned above).

So the answer to the question of Paul's language choice in Acts 21:40 and 22:2, even if given as Hebrew, should be qualified, though not for taxonomic reasons. 'Sociolinguistic eavesdropping' requires attention to domain (here: the Jewish temple precinct), formality (public though impromptu speech) and topic (defense of teaching legitimacy); while this situation might call for Hebrew as the most compelling mode of address, the tension between the ideal and the practicalities of easy comprehension in Aramaic would surely have been reflected in Paul's actual speech, even as the evidence of the specifics would be minimized or erased by its summation in Greek. Conflicting situational needs are discussed in Stewart's 1962 Caribbean study, which shows the complex interaction of (in-)formality and public/private factors and the resulting competition between social factors. Even the subsequent accounts in Acts of Paul's defense before the Sanhedrin (23:1–10), forensic review with Tertullus (24:1–23), and appearances before Festus (25:1–27) and Agrippa II (26:1–32), all present these domain-related complexities that surely required linguistic flexibility and adeptness reminiscent of Robertson's ascription of a "consummate skill and marvelous vividness and dramatic power" on the part of the New Testament's players.

All this leads naturally to Wardhaugh's observation that "it is not uncommon to find references to Standard English being a dialect—admittedly, a very important one—of English . . . " even though the term *dialect* usually implies a local, *non*-standard variety, often an "informal, lower-class or rural speech." He broadens the scope further, adding

> We can observe too that questions such as 'Which language do you speak?' or 'Which dialect do you speak?' may be answered quite differently by people who appear to speak in an identical manner. As Gumperz . . . has pointed out, many regions of the world provide plenty of evidence for what he calls "a bewildering array of language and dialect divisions."[34]

Wardhaugh insists that "socio-historical factors play a crucial role in determining [linguistic] boundaries," alluding to ragged edges of language nomenclature mentioned also by Bell:

> [R]esearch into code-switching demands that we begin not with identifying the two languages but with the overall linguistic practices of the speakers. What language they are speaking may not be the important question—may not even be answerable . . . [since certain speakers] often blend their two languages together in ways that make it unclear which language a particular item belongs to—it may be either or both . . . . Language is a social practice, a range of resources on which speakers draw rather than a set of linguistic 'codes' . . . .[35]

Similarly, Julie Coleman contends that even "[s]tandard English is not a well-defined concept in itself; its meaning varies according to geographical location and social context. Slang, of course, is even harder to define."[36] Daniel Heller-Roazen relates these dynamics even to the cryptic cant of criminals: "In private or in public, those who speak a language retain the capacity to draw from their knowledge of its grammar the elements of a new and cryptic variety of speech."[37]

Today, rapidity of contact and the proliferation of various kinds of media amidst routine communication acts are rendering the face of language perpetually malleable, as in John

34. Wardhaugh, *Introduction to Sociolinguistics*, 24.

35. Bell, *Guidebook to Sociolinguistics*, 31–32, and referencing Peter Auer.

36. Coleman, ed., *Global English Slang*, 1.

37. Heller-Roazen, *Dark Tongues*, 17.

McWhorter's metaphor of language as an ever-morphing lava lamp. Samples of formal bilingual writing intended for public domain (which is not as variable as speech) which I have collected in the past two years in Austria, Germany and Turkey likewise evidence an astonishing diversity of inter-language penetration that includes block translation, word-by-word code-switching, affixation of one language's inflectional or derivational morpheme onto the words of another, not to mention the customary loanwords and loan-blends. Yet these pale in comparison to personal notes provided by a Korean woman raised in Japan who speaks fluent English: though taken in a North American lecture setting, her notes are intermingled with Japanese Hiragana and Katakana scripts, Chinese-origin Kanji symbols and Korean words, along with some Greek word translations. What is the language of her personal notes? The answer may reside in the cultural background of the labeler, for if there are "fifty ways to leave your lover" there's even more by which to leave your mono-lingualism. Languages in contact, especially genetically related ones, evidence interpenetration of lexicon and morpho-syntactic features, and live harmoniously with Hugo Schuchardt's maxim that *Es gibt keine voellig ungemischte Sprache* (There is no completely unmixed language). Formality *and* flexibility both demand a seat at the speech table. Though we cannot eavesdrop on Paul's speech, we can assume that "the linguistic chemistry and dynamics"[38] warranted by circumstantial particulars would have prompted Paul to harness his Semitic resources deftly.

6. *Post-Script*

Language makes a fine tool but a terrible master. Saint Augustine in his *Confessions* prayed "O Lord my God, be patient . . . with the men of this world as you watch them and see how strictly they obey the rules of grammar which have been handed down to

38. Ong, "Linguistic Analysis," 3.

them, and yet ignore the eternal rules of everlasting salvation."[39] Sociolinguists salivate when speech rules are broken, and though the academic study of language-in-context is fairly recent, sociology of language has a long and ignoble history. It was practiced when east-bank Gileadites who were aligned with Jephthah interrogated fleeing west-bank Ephraimites on their pronunciation of *shibboleth* 'ear of corn' (Judg 12:5–6). The slightest of phonetic variation between /*s*/ and /*sh*/—the mere absence of phonetic frication—prompted bloodshed, and in that account (as Christina Paulston likes to say) lies the first recorded case of *applied* sociolinguistics. In 1302, according to some claims, that tradition was continued as Flemish forces identified Frenchmen living in Bruges on the basis of their idiosyncratic pronunciation of the Flemish phrase *schilt ende vriend* 'shield and friend', and slaughtered them. In 1937, suspected Haitian immigrants living along the border with the Dominican Republic were also given impromptu speech 'tests' aimed at identifying vernacular pronunciation of the Spanish word *perejil* 'parsley' and, by order of the president of the Dominican Republic, Haitians were executed in what came to be known as the 'Parsley Massacre.' During World War II, American soldiers in the Pacific quizzed suspected Japanese soldiers on their pronunciation of *lollapalooza*, capitalizing on the common Asian /r~l/ allophonic distribution; at war's end, Dutch patriots trapped fleeing German soldiers by eliciting their pronunciation of the initial consonant cluster in the seaside town of *Scheveningen*.

Today, *Shibboleth*—as the company website explains its name—is an "open source project that provides Single Sign-On capabilities and allows sites to make informed authorization decisions for individual access of protected on-line resources in a privacy-preserving manner."[40] From the Antonia to the internet, the horizon of sociolinguistics has cast quite a long shadow.

39. Cited in Hitchings, *Language Wars*, 25.
40. Shibboleth Consortium, *Shibboleth*. Online: https://shibboleth.net.

Bibliography

Bakhtin, M.M. "Discourse in the Novel." In *The Dialogic Imagination*, edited by Michael Holquist, translated by Caryl Emerson and Michael Holquist, 259–422. Austin: University of Texas Press, 1981.

Baltes, Guido. "The Origins of the 'Exclusive Aramaic Model' in the Nineteenth Century: Methodological Fallacies and Subtle Motives." In *The Language Environment of First Century Judaea*, edited by Randall Buth and R. Steven Notley, 9–34. Jerusalem Studies in the Synoptic Gospels 2. Leiden: Brill, 2014.

_______. "The Use of Hebrew and Aramaic in Epigraphic Sources of the New Testament Era." In *The Language Environment of First Century Judaea*, edited by Randall Buth and R. Steven Notley, 35–65. Jerusalem Studies in the Synoptic Gospels 2. Leiden: Brill, 2014.

Bell, Allan. *The Guidebook to Sociolinguistics*. Chichester, UK: Wiley-Blackwell, 2014.

Buth, Randall. "The Riddle of Jesus' Cry from the Cross: The Meaning of ηλι ηλι λαμα σαβαχθανι (Matthew 27:46) and the Literary Function of ελωι ελωι λειμα σαβαχθανι (Mark 15:34)." In *The Language Environment of First Century Judaea*, edited by Randall Buth and R. Steven Notley, 395–421. Jerusalem Studies in the Synoptic Gospels 2. Leiden: Brill, 2014.

Buth, Randall, and Brian Kvasnica. "Temple Authorities and Tithe Evasion: The Linguistic Background and Impact of the Parable of the Vineyard, the Tenants and the Son." In *Jesus' Last Week*, edited by R. Steven Notley et al., 53–80. Jerusalem Studies in the Synoptic Gospels 1. Leiden: Brill, 2006.

Buth, Randall, and Chad Pierce. "*Hebraisti* in Ancient Texts: Does Ἑβραϊστί Ever Mean 'Aramaic'?" In *The Language Environment of First Century Judaea*, edited by Randall Buth and R. Steven Notley, 66–109. Jerusalem Studies in the Synoptic Gospels 2. Leiden: Brill, 2014.

Canagarajah, A. Suresh. *Resisting Linguistic Imperialism in English Teaching*. Oxford: Oxford University Press, 1999.

Coleman, Julie, ed. *Global English Slang: Methodologies and Perspectives*. New York: Routledge, 2014.

Eshel, Hanan. "Use of the Hebrew Language in Economic Documents from the Judaean Desert." In *Jesus' Last Week*, edited by R. Steven

Notley et al., 245–58. Jerusalem Studies in the Synoptic Gospels 1. Leiden: Brill, 2006.

Fitzmyer, Joseph A. *The Semitic Background of the New Testament: Volume II: A Wandering Aramean: Collected Aramaic Essays*. Grand Rapids: Eerdmans, 1997.

Heller-Roazen, Daniel. *Dark Tongues: The Art of Rogues and Riddlers*. New York: Zone Books, 2013.

Hitchings, Henry. *The Language Wars*. New York: Farrar, Strauss and Giroux, 2011.

Hudson, R.A. *Sociolinguistics*. 2nd ed. Cambridge: Cambridge University Press, 1996.

Kachru, Braj B. "Teaching World Englishes." In *The Other Tongue: English across Cultures*, 355–65. 2nd ed. Urbana, IL: University of Illinois Press, 1992.

Kuhn, K.G. "Ἰσραήλ, Ἰουδαῖος, Ἑβραῖος in Jewish Literature after the OT." *TDNT* 3:359–69.

Millard, Alan. *Reading and Writing in the Time of Jesus*. Sheffield: Sheffield Academic, 2000.

Ong, Hughson. "Can Linguistic Analysis in Historical Jesus Research Stand on its Own? A Sociolinguistic Analysis of Matthew 26:36—27:26." *BAGL* 2 (2013) 109–38.

Romaine, Suzanne. *Language in Society*. 2nd ed. Oxford: Oxford University Press, 2000.

Ruzer, Serge. "Hebrew versus Aramaic as Jesus' Language: Notes on Early Opinions by Syriac Authors." In *The Language Environment of First Century Judaea*, edited by Randall Buth and R. Steven Notley, 182–206. Jerusalem Studies in the Synoptic Gospels 2. Leiden: Brill, 2014.

Safrai, Shmuel. "Spoken and Literary Languages in the Time of Jesus." In *Jesus' Last Week*, edited by R. Steven Notley et al., 225–44. Jerusalem Studies in the Synoptic Gospels 1. Leiden: Brill, 2006.

Stewart, William A. "An Outline of Linguistic Typology for Describing Multilingualism." In *Study of the Role of Second Languages in Asia, Africa and Latin America*, edited by F.A. Rice, 15–25. Washington, DC: Center for Applied Linguistics, 1962.

_______. "Creole languages of the Caribbean." In *Study of the Role of Second Languages in Asia, Africa and Latin America*, edited by F.A. Rice, 34–52. Washington, DC: Center for Applied Linguistics, 1962.

Wallace, Daniel B. *Greek Grammar beyond the Basics*. Grand Rapids: Zondervan, 1996.

Wardhaugh, Ronald. *An Introduction to Sociolinguistics*. 3rd ed. Chichester, UK: Blackwell, 1998.

Watt, Jonathan. "Some Implications of Bilingualism for New Testament Exegesis." In *The Language of the New Testament: Context, History, and Development*, edited by Stanley E. Porter and Andrew W. Pitts, 9–27. Early Christianity in Its Hellenistic Context 3. Linguistic Biblical Studies 6. Leiden: Brill, 2013.

_______. "A Brief History of Ancient Greek with a View to the New Testament." In *The Language of the New Testament: Context, History, and Development*, edited by Stanley E. Porter and Andrew W. Pitts, 225–41. Early Christianity in Its Hellenistic Context 3. Linguistic Biblical Studies 6. Leiden: Brill, 2013.

[*BAGL* 4 (2015) 49–84]

Sociolinguistics and New Testament Exegesis: Three Approaches to Discourse Analysis Using Acts 21:27—22:5 as a Test Case[1]

Hughson T. Ong
McMaster Divinity College, Hamilton, ON, Canada

Abstract: This article discusses three distinct types of discourse analysis models—Social Identity Theory and Communication Accommodation Theory (CAT), Conversation Analysis (CA), and SFL Register Analysis—and applies them individually to the text in Acts 21:27—22:5 to examine various aspects and elements that comprise the context of situation of the incident of Paul's arrest in the temple. The main objective is to showcase the relevance and utility of sociolinguistic theories in New Testament exegesis. (Article)

Keywords: Acts 21:27—22:5, sociolinguistics, exegesis, discourse analysis, social identity theory, speech or communication accommodation theory, conversation analysis, register analysis.

1. *Introduction*

Exegesis continues to be an important component and mundane activity in New Testament studies—it is what keeps the business running.[2] To start talking about exegesis, however, is often a challenging task, for it can involve a complex discussion of a number of interrelated issues—the nature, problems, and history

1. This article was originally an invited conference paper presented at the annual meeting of the Evangelical Theological Society (New Testament Greek Language and Exegesis Consultation) in San Diego, California, USA on 19 November 2014.
2. Cf. Conzelmann and Lindemann, *Interpreting the New Testament*, 1.

of exegesis,[3] the various methods of exegesis,[4] and even the debate over the term "exegesis."[5] It is not my intention to get involved in such discussions, but I want to acknowledge these issues to recognize the complexities involved in dealing with the topic of New Testament exegesis. It is also not my intention to critique other types of exegetical methods. My intention is rather to demonstrate the relevance and utility of sociolinguistic theories for the exegetical task. Specifically, I wish to show that sociolinguistic theories can provide us with the best tools for analyzing the text of the New Testament, as these theories have the means to account for the dynamic interplay of the three components—language, people, and society—that make up the situational contexts behind the text of the New Testament. This article has three major sections. The first section defines, in sociolinguistic terms, the meaning of text and context, and explains the relation of these two terms to the concept of register (or standard and variable social domains). The second section discusses three sociolinguistic approaches to analyzing the text of the New Testament. The third and last section then demonstrates how these three approaches can be applied to the text in Acts 21:27—22:5 (Paul's Arrest in the temple). Before I turn to the first section, some parameters of this study are in order.

3. An excellent resource on the history of New Testament interpretation is Baird, *History of New Testament Research*.

4. On methods of New Testament interpretation, see Hayes and Holladay, *Biblical Exegesis*, 73–82, 110–30; Black and Dockery, eds., *Interpreting the New Testament*, 2–186; McKnight and Osborne, eds., *The Face of New Testament Studies*, 59–145; and Green, ed., *Hearing the New Testament*.

5. New Testament studies have already moved beyond the period of traditional historical exegesis (or grammatico-historical exegesis). Exegesis of this type typically requires the reader to focus the exegetical task and activity upon determining the historical background and the original author's and audience's intentions in order to discover the meaning of the text (see Kümmel, *The New Testament*, 111–12; Fee, *New Testament Exegesis*, 27; Marshall, ed., *New Testament Interpretation*, 220, 252; and Marshall, "The Problem of New Testament Exegesis," 67–73. For a summative discussion as well as a critique of traditional exegesis, see Porter and Clarke, "What Is Exegesis," 3–21.

First, I note that the term "exegesis" needs to be distinguished from the term "hermeneutics." Whereas exegesis is the application of hermeneutical theories to the interpretation of texts, hermeneutics refers to the science of formulating guidelines, rules, and methods for interpretation or the ways in which we may theorize about human interpretation.[6] Second, I emphasize the importance and priority of one's goal of investigation in the exegetical process; the ultimate goal of exegesis is to provide the best answer to the question asked in the investigation of a particular New Testament text. Thus, each individual textual analysis of Acts 21:27—22:5 in the third section of this article is constrained by a specific question that it seeks to answer. Third and last, as already mentioned, my focus is upon demonstrating how sociolinguistic theories can be applied to the text of the New Testament. I am not positing any particular argument for the interpretation of our passage of interest. My interpretation of the text in Acts 21:27—22:5 as a result of my sociolinguistic analyses, however, can certainly either clarify or supplement previous interpretations of the passage.

2. *Text, Context, and Register (Standard and Variable Domain Concepts)*

The traditional definition of "text" and "context" in New Testament exegesis is that the former refers to "what is said" (content) in a given New Testament text or document, and the latter refers to "why it is said" (context). The latter, context, is expressed in terms of historical context, which indicates the historical, sociocultural, and occasional nature of a New Testament document, and in terms of literary context, which denotes the reason why a given text was said at a particular point

6. Exegesis is sometimes taken as a synonym for hermeneutics and interpretation (see Porter and Clarke, "What Is Exegesis," 4–6). On the topic of hermeneutics, see Porter and Robinson, *Hermeneutics*; Thiselton, *The Two Horizons*; and *idem*, *Hermeneutics*.

in the document. To get at these two contexts is to get at the author's intended meaning.[7] In sociolinguistic terms, however, these concepts or terms are defined in a different manner.

2.1 *Text as Discourse or Conversation*

Sociolinguists have given various definitions to the terms "text" and "context," but it is helpful to start with a particular definition of text and work our way towards a definition of the concepts of context and register. Brown and Yule define text as "the verbal record of a communicative act."[8] Two important notions are immediately apparent in this definition. On the one hand, a "verbal record" implies that a text is composed of a word or a string of words that is subsequently governed by the lexico-grammatical rules and features of a particular language. On the other hand, a "communicative act" indicates that a text is actually an instance of social and linguistic interaction, whether written (text) or spoken (conversation).[9] The story of Paul's arrest in the temple in Acts 21:27—22:5 is an instance of sociolinguistic interaction or a discourse between the author and the audience of the book of Acts. Similarly, the embedded conversation found in Acts 21:37–39 is also an instance of sociolinguistic interaction between Paul and the cohort commander (χιλίαρχος).

2.2 *Context (Context of Situation) and Register*

The social situation or context within which a linguistic interaction comes to life is called the context of situation or the situational context.[10] More specifically, a context of situation is a situation type that can be identified within the social structure or system of a particular community or society. The aggregate number of the situation types found in a real community

7. Fee, *New Testament Exegesis*, 5.
8. Brown and Yule, *Discourse Analysis*, 6, 190.
9. See Halliday, *Language and Society*, 179–80.
10. Goodwin and Duranti note four dimensions of context that sociolinguists explore: setting, behavioral environment, language as context, and extra-situational context ("Rethinking Context," 6–9).

constitutes, in social terms, its context of culture, and, in linguistic terms, the entire semantic system of a particular language.[11] A situation type is also a semiotic structure, which means that it can be represented by a set of linguistic elements that configure or describe that situation type. The linguistic configuration of a particular social interaction in a discourse or conversation is known as register. Register is a concept often used in sociolinguistics to differentiate between language variation according to its user (dialect) and language variation according to its use (register).[12] Dialect is used to categorize different groups of people that speak different languages within a language community. Register, by contrast, is a means to categorize language according to its various uses; it is a powerful concept that can account for what people do with their language. M.A.K. Halliday notes that, because it is difficult to identify the registers of a language on the basis of their formal properties, it is therefore helpful to distinguish registers from the perspective of institutional linguistics, since "There is enough evidence for us to be able to recognize the major situation types to which formally distinct registers correspond."[13] Register analysis is one of the sociolinguistic approaches that attempt to define the context of situation of a social or linguistic interaction, a subject that I will return to below. In the meantime, I will introduce a new concept that could further elucidate the concept of register.

11. Halliday, *Language and Society*, 180–81.

12. See Hudson, *Sociolinguistics*, 45–49; Holmes, *Introduction*, 259–64, who compares register with style, noting that the former is usually analyzed along a scale of formality; she also notes vocabulary choice, syntactic reduction, syntactic inversion, routines and formulas, and heavy noun modification as some of the elements that may distinguish one register from another; and Halliday, *Language and Society*, 16–26, 181–82. On the use of these concepts in New Testament studies, see Porter, "Dialect and Register"; and "Register in the Greek of the New Testament," 190–229.

13. Halliday, *Language and Society*, 19.

2.3 *Standard and Variable Domain*[14]

The concept of social or language domain is not entirely new in that the concept has already been used in sociolinguistic studies.[15] Domains refer to a set of institutionalized contexts that involve "typical interactions between typical participants in typical settings."[16] These institutionalized contexts, such as family, friendship, religion, education, government, transaction, employment, etc. can be found in *virtually* all speech communities. As such, in sociolinguistic terms, it is perhaps helpful to call them standard (or fixed domains). Within each standard domain of a particular speech community, however, we observe that there are many specific situational contexts that can be observed. I call these situational contexts variable domains, since, while we can say that they still fall under a specific standard domain, they deviate in various ways from the typicality of the sociolinguistic components (e.g., participants, setting, purpose, message form, message content, etc.) that configure standard domains.

This bifurcation of social or language domains into standard and variable domains is an important concept for three reasons. First, it brings the concepts of context of culture (something that cannot be described) and context of situation (something that can evolve into an infinite number of situation types) closer to each other,[17] providing an intermediate bridge between context of situation and context of culture. Second, it allows for a clearer identification of a specific register, since, while each context of situation is, strictly speaking, always unique (cf. the concept of

14. I first introduce the concept of standard and variable domains in Ong, *Multilingual Jesus*, especially chs. 4 and 5.

15. The origin of this concept can be attributed to the work of Fishman ("Micro- and Macro-Sociolinguistics," 22). Cf. Ferguson, "Diglossia," 28. On the application of the domain concept in New Testament studies, see Ong, "Language Choice in Ancient Palestine," 63–101; and especially, *idem*, *Multilingual Jesus*, esp. 122–3, 258–9.

16. Holmes, *Introduction*, 21.

17. Halliday, *Language and Society*, 180, notes that the concepts of context of culture and context of situation are both "fictional" in the sense that they can only operate in the abstract.

idiolect for language users), it nevertheless can be classified into one of the standard domains or larger social institutions of a speech community. Third, by using these two complementary concepts, we can now move from an abstract description of the context of situation to a more concrete and realistic one. This is something that the concept of register is not able to do, at least when used in New Testament exegesis. To be sure, for the purpose of New Testament exegesis, it is important that we analyze and describe the context of situation of a text over and against its larger social contexts, that is, those institutionalized contexts that actually existed in the speech community of the first century CE.

In summary, in sociolinguistic terms, a given text in the New Testament is treated not simply as the "content" (what is said) of a document. Rather, the text is treated as a "situated text." A text in sociolinguistic terms is a situated text, since its production entails a context of situation, a situation type that can be identified within the larger social contexts or institutions of a particular community.[18] Context of situation is different from "context" (why the content is said) as defined in traditional exegesis. Context of situation is a description and a configuration of the exchanges of meanings of the participants in the sociolinguistic interaction expressed through the text, that is, the social environment of the text. To describe the context of situation of a text requires an analysis of its register or language domain in order to identify the situation type or variable domain type of the text.

Applying these concepts to the text in Acts 21:27—22:5, we can see that the passage is a type of discourse between its author and audience. In that discourse, the author narrates an historical account, that is, the incident concerning Paul's arrest in the temple. To provide a descriptive analysis of the various sociolinguistic factors (i.e., message, purpose, participants, setting, topic, etc.) that are at play in this incident of Paul's arrest in the temple, we need a systematic methodological approach to

18. This notion is usually attributed to the work of Malinowski ("Meaning in Primitive Languages," 306).

analyze the discourse. Similarly, we may also consider Paul's conversation with the cohort commander as a distinct discourse embedded within the larger discourse of Paul's arrest in the temple, and analysis of that embedded discourse in detail also requires the same systematic methodological approach. There are at least three systematic methodological approaches to analyzing a discourse.

3. *Three Sociolinguistic Approaches to Analyzing a Text (or Discourse)*

In the previous section, I differentiated the meaning of text and context as used in sociolinguistics from its use in traditional historical exegesis. Sociolinguists define text as a "situated text," that is, a text produced from a context of situation, an identifiable type of social situation (variable domain) within a larger social context (standard domain) of a particular speech community. It is in this complementary relationship between a text and its context of situation that we are able to see the utility and strength of sociolinguistics for the exegetical task. I will note three reasons why sociolinguistics serves as a useful tool for New Testament exegesis. First, the discipline is an amalgamation of various disciplines from the social sciences, notably sociology (the study of human society and its development, structure, and functions), anthropology (the study of humans and their sociocultural values and behavior), and linguistics (the study of language and its structure and use),[19] making sociolinguistics effectually the study of the interdependent relationship of people, language, and society. These three sociolinguistic elements are the necessary components for the production of texts, and one cannot (meaningfully) exist without the other two. Second, sociolinguistics is able to establish a clear and formal linkage between a text and its context as I have pointed out in the preceding section. Third, sociolinguistics has the theoretical

19. For a discussion of the theoretical convergence of these three disciplines in sociolinguistics, see Shuy, "A Brief History," 11–32.

capacity to provide a more robust explanation as to why people speak and behave in particular ways in a particular culture. Language use follows the set of social norms, not just the rules of grammar, of a particular speech community.

Given these strengths and the usefulness of sociolinguistics as a tool for New Testament exegesis, there are at least three methodological approaches to analyzing a particular text or discourse. Each of these three approaches comprises a number of discourse analytic tools that focus on any of the three sociolinguistic elements that produce a text. First, analysis may be focused on the individuals or social agents that are involved in the discourse, searching for ways to explain why they are doing what they are doing (e.g., social identity theory, communication accommodation theory, language and social psychology approaches). Second, analysis may be concentrated on the instance of text or discourse (whether spoken, written, or signed text) that unfolds in a particular context, examining the micro-interactional features of the text, such as structure, patterns, cues, and other background features (e.g., conversation analysis, critical discourse analysis, interactional socio-linguistics). Third, analysis may be approached in terms of a systemic framework expressed both in social terms as a form of interpersonal behavior and in semiotic terms as an exchange of meaning and knowledge (e.g., Systemic Functional Linguistics).[20] In what follows, I select and discuss a discourse analytic tool for each of these three approaches.

20. There is a fourth approach, that is, by theorizing and describing the text as a system or potential that contains propositional meaning (e.g., speech act theory, conversational implicature, language pragmatics). This approach, however, encroaches upon the field of philosophy; it thus falls outside the purview of my discussion here, although many introductions to sociolinguistics and literature on linguistic pragmatics still include them in the discussion (see Goodwin and Duranti, "Rethinking Context," 13–31; Matthiessen and Slade, "Analysing Conversation," 378; and Edwards, "Discursive Psychology," 257–73.

3.1 *Social Identity Theory and Communication Accommodation Theory (Social Agent Focused)*

One of the main applications of Social Identity theory and Communication Accommodation Theory (CAT) in socio-linguistics is in studying intergroup behavior, and more specifically, in determining the solidarity relationship between the participants in a linguistic interaction within a particular context of situation.[21] Participants are perhaps the most important component in a social interaction, for without this component, a social interaction cannot take place. Henri Tajfel was the first to introduce the term "social identity," and he defined the term as "that part of the individual's self concept which derives from their knowledge of their membership of a social group (or groups) together with the value and emotional significance attached to that membership."[22] Tajfel's point is that individuals project a public face in a social interaction according to *how* they want their interaction partners to view them, and generally, people prefer a positive to a negative public face.[23] There are two parts of "face": one part is concerned with the interpersonal relationship between participants, and the other part is concerned with the social classification of the speaker. Accommodation theory (see below) posits that when a speaker likes their interaction partners (interpersonal relations), they naturally will want to become *like* them (social classification).[24]

According to Richard Hudson, the solidarity relationship is the most salient of all social relationships, as it reflects shared experiences through the use of similar language or linguistic codes.[25] A solidarity relationship is assessed using the so-called "social-distance dimension scale," a scale that measures participants' relationship of more or less "equal" status. Friendly relations move along this dimension scale, and they are signaled

21. On the application of these theories to Mark 14:32–65, see Ong, "An Evaluation," 37–55.

22. Tajfel, *Social Identity*, 2.

23. Tajfel, *Human Groups and Social Categories*, 45.

24. Hudson, *Sociolinguistics*, 239.

25. Hudson, *Sociolinguistics*, 232.

by the absence of superior-subordinate linguistic codes, such as use of titles and honorifics, formal politeness language (e.g., linguistic forms of requests), and deferential gestures or behaviors. In creating a positive public face, people typically "accommodate" their behavior and speech to that of their interaction partners.

Howard Giles developed accommodation theory, when he explored some of the cognitive reasons for conversational code-switching. Giles notes that his theory derives from social identity principles and observes that people either "converge to" or "diverge from" their interaction partners depending upon their social goals and motivations.[26] Participants either "reduce" or "increase" differences in behavior or speech in order to stress their solidarity relationship. As such, accommodation behavior comes in two types. A convergence behavior happens when participants like each other, when they want to gain social approval by sacrificing something (e.g., their public face or right to something),[27] or when they have an interest vested in their interaction partners.[28] Participants may also adopt the accent, dialect, or language of their interaction partners.[29] By contrast, a divergence behavior happens when participants want to break away from the behavior of their interaction partners, when they want to be judged negatively, or when they want to be seen as uncooperative or antagonistic.[30] On the basis of these principles, accommodation theory, therefore, can be used to explain how

26. See Giles and Coupland, *Language*, 60–1; and Giles and Street, "Speech Accommodation Theory," 193–226.

27. Wardhaugh, *Introduction*, 114.

28. Holmes, *Introduction*, 242.

29. One important question analysts using accommodation theory must ask is whether people are accommodating linguistically (i.e., making speech more similar to one's interaction partner) or socially (i.e., matching one's social status to that of one's interaction partner). See Coupland, "Accommodation at Work," 65; and Hudson, *Sociolinguistics*, 164–66.

30. See Holmes, *Introduction*, 232–33; and Wardhaugh, *Introduction*, 114. For a list of the types of dissociative situations where people accentuate their differences between themselves and others, see Street and Giles, "Speech Accommodation Theory," 208.

participants relate to each other,[31] and on such basis determine their social goals and motivations in a particular context of situation.

3.2 *Conversation Analysis (Text Focused)*

If social identity theory and communication accommodation theory is participant focused, Conversation Analysis (CA) is text focused or discourse focused. If participants are an inevitable component in a social interaction, the use of language expressed in terms of spoken or written texts is an equally important component. Conversation analysis originated from the work of a group of sociologists—Harvey Sacks, Emanuel Schegloff, and Gail Jefferson—who collaborated to provide a theoretical concept that attempts at discovering and explaining why mundane conversations make sense, presupposing conversation or discourse as a body of situated texts or social practices.[32] The conversation analysis model developed by this group of sociologists was assessed for its compatibility with a list of what they called "grossly observable facts"[33] in any type of

31. Wardhaugh, *Introduction*, 114.

32. See Drew, "Conversation Analysis," 75; Sacks et al., "Simplest Systematics," 696–735; and Sacks, "Initial Investigation," 31–74.

33. There are fourteen observable facts: "(1) Speaker-change recurs, or at least occurs; (2) Overwhelmingly, one party talks at a time; (3) Occurrences of more than one speaker at a time are common, but brief; (4) Transitions (from one turn to a next) with no gap and no overlap are common. Together with transitions characterized by slight gap or slight overlap, they make up the vast majority of transitions; (5) Turn order is not fixed, but varies; (6) Turn size is not fixed, but varies; (7) Length of conversation is not specified in advance; (8) What parties say is not specified in advance; (9) Relative distribution of turns is not specified in advance; (10) Number of parties can vary; (11) Talk can be continuous or discontinuous; (12) Turn-allocation techniques are obviously used. A current speaker may select a next speaker (as when he addresses a question to another party); or parties may self-select in starting a talk; (13) Various 'turn-constructional units' are employed; e.g., turns can be projectedly 'one word long,' or they can be sentential in length; and (14) Repair mechanisms exist for dealing with turn-taking errors and violations; e.g., if two parties find themselves talking at the same time, one of them will stop prematurely, thus repairing the trouble" (Sacks et al., "Simplest Systematics,"

conversation.[34] For this reason, conversation analysis serves as a useful tool for analyzing all forms of genres of talk-in-interaction from institutional talks to the larger, diverse field of communications.

Because it is text focused, conversation analysis only makes use of and pays attention to the information available in the text, without referring to extra-textual ethnographic information.[35] The utility and strength of this discourse analytic model is thus seen in its ability to analyze the relationship, structure, patterns, and sequence organization of text. There are three major concepts involved in analyzing a text that uses conversation analysis.[36] The first one is turn-taking. Speakers take turns in speaking: the current speaker selects the next speaker or the next speaker self-selects or the current speaker continues speaking. Turns are realized by what is called turn constructional units (TCU), which is the minimal unit that can constitute one complete turn of talk, which, in turn, can be a word, a phrase, or a sentence.

The second concept is turn action and design. Speakers decide on the performative action (e.g., invitation, elicitation, command or request, offer, rejection, etc.) of their turn and the verbal construction (lexical choice, grammatical construction, and non-verbal aspects) through which the action will be accomplished. The assumption of this concept is that speakers construct their turn in a conversation to fit into what comes before it; hence, the corollary assumption that participants in any normal, mundane social interaction are typically able to understand each other in a conversation. A deviation from this norm needs explanation and interpretation.

700–701).

34. It is important to note that there are many models of conversation analysis. One prominent model is that of John Sinclair and Malcolm Coulthard who developed their conversation analysis model based on Hallidayan Systemic Functional Linguistics (see Sinclair and Coulthard, *Towards an Analysis of Discourse*; and Coulthard, *Introduction*, 52–115).

35. Holmes, *Introduction*, 381.

36. For a discussion of these concepts, see Drew, "Conversation Analysis," 77–99. Cf. Fairclough, *Discourse and Social Change*, 16–20.

The third and last concept is sequence organization. When turns are analyzed in a conversation, they reveal systematically organized sequences of texts. The most basic sequence organization is adjacency pairs—a pair of turns produced by two different speakers. Typical adjacency pairs include question/ answer, complaint/denial, complement/rejection, request/grant, and offer/accept.[37] In a conversation, even though there are many adjacency pairs within it, there is only one so-called base adjacency pair, which serves as the gist or the main topic or concern of the conversation. The other adjacency pairs in such a case, therefore, only serve as expansions of the base adjacency pair. Expansions are expressed in terms of sequences of moves—pre-sequences (expansions preceding the first pair part of the base adjacency pair), insertion sequences and side sequences (expansions within the first and second pair parts of the base adjacency pair), and post-sequences (expansions after the second pair part of the base adjacency pair). Insertion sequences are expansions that are inexplicitly related to the pair part it is expanding (and thus need further explanation and interpretation), whereas side sequences are expansions that explicitly clarify or explain the pair part it is expanding.[38]

3.3 *Register Analysis—Systemic Functional Linguistics (System Network Focused)*

It is perhaps a misnomer to say that register analysis in the tradition of Systemic Functional Linguistics (SFL), with reference to using the model in textual analysis, is focused on a system network and not on the text or discourse itself that is under study. However, I think that this is perhaps the best way to contrast SFL register analysis with other types of discourse analytic models. This notion will become clearer as I discuss this model in what follows. The concept of register has been developed by Hallidayan SFL to provide a systematized network for establishing the formal linkages between a text and its

37. For Sacks's final word on adjacency pairs, see Sacks, *Lectures on Conversation*, 521–75.

38. See Wardhaugh, *Introduction*, 303.

context of situation.[39] The relations of the various sociolinguistic components that comprise this network may be explained in the following manner and order. A text is a social action instantiated in a specific linguistic form or wording (i.e., the lexico-grammatical structure). A text is also a product of various choices of meaning made by a speaker. The social environment in which a text unfolds is the context of situation, an instance of a social context or a situation type. The situation type of a text can also be called its register—the semantic configuration or the characteristics of the situation type.

This situation type is both a semiotic structure (a system of representation of meanings) and a semantic structure (a system of meanings). The semiotic structure of a situation type may be represented in terms of three socio-semiotic variables: (1) field (concerned with the purpose and subject matter of the interaction); (2) tenor (concerned with participants' relations); and (3) mode (concerned with the means and structure by which the linguistic interaction takes place). These socio-semiotic variables are directly related to the semantic structure of the situation type that is represented in terms of three functional components: (1) ideational (represents the "content" function of language); (2) interpersonal (represents the "participation" function of language); and (3) textual (represents the "relevance" function of language, that is, its thematic and informational structure that actualizes the ideational and interpersonal components). It is important to note at this point that, in SFL terms, social function is equivalent to social meaning; the meaning of a text also simultaneously means its social function. For this reason, each socio-semiotic variable corresponds to each

39. The Hallidayan bibliography is large. My discussion here of SFL register analysis follows Halliday, *Explorations*, 22–102; Halliday, *Language as Social Semiotic*, 31–35, 60–64, 130–45, 186–89, 221–27; Halliday, *Language and Society*, 17–26, 93–96, 132–36, 196–200; and Thompson, *Introducing Functional Grammar*. For a summary and critique of Hallidayan linguistics, see Butler, *Systemic Linguistics*, 62–68, 92; and most recently, Porter, "Systemic Functional Linguistics."

of the three functional semantic components; field is realized by the ideational component, tenor by the interpersonal component, and mode by the textual component.

The relationship between these three elements in the language network may be stated as follows: the contextual configuration (field, tenor, and mode) of a situation type is realized semantically by the functional/semantic components (ideational, interpersonal, and textual) of a text that are in turn realized in the lexicogrammar or wording of a text (i.e., context→speech function/meaning→text; thus, speech function or meaning serve as the "bridge" between the text and its context). When analyzing the ideational meanings of a text, we look at the kinds of activities and topics that are talked about, including when, by whom, and how they unfold and are achieved. In other words, we are concerned with the shared experience and view of the world participants construe together. When analyzing its interpersonal meanings, we examine the types of role relationships, attitudes, and various negotiations that are established between participants. Lastly, when analyzing its textual meanings, we are interested in determining how participants structure and manage the information flow of the text in such a way that they are able to guide and understand each other in their exchange.[40]

There are at least three types of analysis involved in examining these three meanings in a text.[41] First, ideational meanings can be discovered through transitivity analysis.[42] Transitivity analysis identifies the participant (the nominal group), the process (the verbal group),[43] and the circumstance

40. Matthiessen and Slade, "Analysing Conversation," 385.

41. There are more types and complex levels of analysis for determining the meanings or functions of each semantic component of a clause in a discourse. For a summative discussion, see Thompson, *Introducing Functional Grammar*, chs. 3–7.

42. Transitivity analysis is analysis of the verbal network of a clause, that is, the verb itself and all the items depending on it (see Halliday, *Introduction to Functional Grammar*, 168–306).

43. There are at least four major types of processes—material, mental, relational, and verbal (Thompson, *Introducing Functional Grammar*, 90–105).

(the adverbial or prepositional group) of a clause and attempts to explain their relationship with other clauses in the text or discourse. In doing so, the analyst can draw conclusions regarding the topic, setting, and goals of a discourse through lexical items (nominal, verbal, and circumstance) that either recur frequently or belong to the same semantic field.

Second, interpersonal meanings are gleaned from mood analysis. If the focus of transitivity analysis is on the "content" of the clause, the focus of mood analysis is on the "interaction" by which the content is negotiated between the participants. The content may be negotiated in terms of a statement (i.e., to offer goods/services or to give information), a question (i.e., to demand information), or a command (i.e., to demand goods/services), all of which are realized and indicated by mood forms, such as indicatives, subjunctives, imperatives, and optatives (or tense forms; for example, in Greek, imperatives may be expressed in future forms). Verbal mood forms can also reveal the social roles of the participants within a particular discourse.

Third and last, textual meanings are derived from analysis of the organization of a text. In addition to the propositions speakers assert about their world and the type of interaction they negotiate with their listeners, speakers also organize their message in such a way that the message fits in with other parts and that their listeners are able to make sense of the message. There are three basic ways in which speakers organize their texts: (1) by lexical (similar wording) and grammatical repetition (similar meaning) to show that parts of a text (not necessarily adjacent to each other) are related in one way or another; (2) by use of conjunctions to show how parts of a text are related; and (3) by thematization (the first constituent of a clause) to indicate the "point of departure of the message."[44] Speakers highlight the point of departure of their message for a reason, that is, to emphasize a point or to highlight a particular aspect in their message.

44. Halliday, *Introduction to Functional Grammar*, 64.

I have discussed briefly in this section three sociolinguistic approaches to analyzing a text or discourse. The discussion is meant to be "introductory" in nature and orientation, as my main objective from the very start has been to demonstrate how sociolinguistics and its theories can be used as a powerful exegetical tool for New Testament exegesis. In this last section that follows, I will show how these theories can be applied to the text of Acts 21:27—22:5.

4. *Applying These Three Methodological Approaches to Acts 21:27—22:5*

As noted above, the priority of the exegetical task is to determine the goal of investigation or to ask the specific question one seeks to answer. Prioritizing the goal of investigation allows one to select the appropriate tool for the particular job. As we have seen above, each of the discourse analytic tools has its own utility and focus in terms of the kinds of goals it can achieve when applied to a text or discourse. Whereas social identity theory and communication theory are typically employed to assess solidarity and power relationships between participants, conversational analysis is used to analyze the patterns, structure, and organization sequence of a text or discourse. Register analysis, on the other hand, is a useful tool for getting at the context of situation of a text, describing the various sociolinguistic components, such as goals, purpose, message, topics, motivations, etc. of the text or discourse. In the following textual analysis, therefore, I will ask a specific question for each of the sociolinguistic theories that I use in applying them to the text in Acts 21:27—22:5.

4.1 *Analyzing the Social Relationship between Paul and the Crowd in Acts 21:27—22:5 (Social Identity Theory and Communication Accommodation Theory)*

The text (or discourse) in Acts 21:27—22:5 commences with a group of Jews from Asia stirring up a crowd and seizing Paul from the temple area (21:27). The reasons for Paul's arrest may be gleaned from the texts in 21:28–29, 34, 36, and 22:2–5. It is important to observe that the accusation of the Jews was not an insignificant one for three obvious social actions that happened in the incident. First, the Jews not only tried to arrest (ἐπιβάλλω) Paul (21:27, 30), but they also attempted to kill (ἀποκτείνω) and destroy (αἴρω) him (21:31, 36). Second, even though it was probably part of their tactical plan to stir up (συγχέω) the crowd (21:27, 30, 31, 34, 35), they actually persuaded the crowd and set them in a violent (βία) rioting (κινέω; θόρυβος) (21:30, 31, 34, 35).[45] Third, the author of Acts says that the cohort commander and his soldiers had to intervene because of the violent commotion in the city (21:31–35). It is also interesting to observe that, while these violent social actions were happening, the text does not indicate Paul's reaction to the crowd until 21:37, when Paul had the chance to ask permission from the cohort commander to address the crowd. In fact, the text does not even mention any kind of resistance at all to the violence that was inflicted upon him by the crowd. While we may logically speculate that Paul would naturally have resisted and fought against or escaped from such a kind of violence from his assailants, this might have been what actually happened in the light of his address to the crowd in 22:2–5. Several aspects of his testimonial speech to the crowd show that Paul was converging to his assailants, despite their accusation and their violence inflicted upon him. I will note these aspects in his testimonial speech, after examining the accusations of his assailants. This will allow us to see more clearly that Paul actually did converge and accommodate himself to his assailants' accusations.

We find the accusations of Paul's assailants in the very first incident in 21:28–29. The Jews from Asia accuse Paul of teaching things against their people, their law, and their place (ὁ κατὰ τοῦ λαοῦ καὶ τοῦ νόμου καὶ τοῦ τόπου) and of bringing Trophimus the Ephesian into the temple.[46] The second incident is

45. The terms κινέω, θόρυβος, and συγχέω (i.e., its noun cognate σύγχυσις), which, respectively, mean, "to start a riot," "riot," and "to stir up" all belong to the semantic sub-domain "riot" (see Louw and Nida, *Lexicon*, 1:497–98).

46. Bringing Gentiles into the prohibited areas of the temple courts is a

found in 21:34–36. It is unclear what the crowd was actually saying at this point, for they were telling the cohort commander different things concerning Paul, causing the commander "to fail in getting at the truth of the matter" (*μὴ δυναμένου δὲ αὐτοῦ γνῶναι τὸ ἀσφαλὲς*) (21:34). All the crowd wants was "to get rid of him" (*αἶρε αὐτόν*) (21:36). In response to these things, Paul secures permission from the cohort commander to speak to the people (21:37–40). Paul, "having set himself up on the steps" (ἑστὼς ἐπὶ τῶν ἀναβαθμῶν), gave a signal with his hand to the crowd (*κατέσεισεν τῇ χειρὶ τῷ λαῷ*), and spoke to them in Aramaic (*προσεφώνησεν τῇ Ἑβραΐδι διαλέκτῳ*). Contrary to F.F. Bruce's assertion that Paul's gesture of his hand indicated Luke's intention to demonstrate the power of Paul's personality, the hand gesture was probably simply a typical way that people act when they are about to address a (noisy) crowd to obtain silence from their audience (cf. 21:40, *πολλῆς δὲ σιγῆς γενομένης*).[47] What is perhaps more significant is Luke's use of the perfect active participle ἑστὼς (ἵστημι) in the verse. Luke might have wanted to frontground or emphasize the action of Paul as someone speaking from an authoritative standpoint.[48]

The first evidence of linguistic accommodation on Paul's part, however, was his use of the Aramaic language (21:40).[49] That the

capital offense, and death was the penalty of the offense. Two inscriptional notices were discovered in 1871 and in 1935, which had this inscribed text: "No foreigner may enter within the barricade which surrounds the temple and enclosure. Anyone who is caught trespassing will bear personal responsibility for his ensuing death" (see Clermont-Ganneau, "Herod's Temple," 132–33; and Illife, "ΘΑΝΑΤΟΣ Inscription," 1–3).

47. Bruce, *Acts*, 413.

48. On the concept of verbal aspect in the use of the Greek tense-forms, see Porter, *Verbal Aspect*, 75–109, esp. 91–93; and *idem*, *Idioms*, 20–26.

49. I wish to note here that, with reference to the linguistic situation of Palestine, there are many conclusions that we can glean from this passage. One is that first-century Palestine was to a certain degree (on the basis of this incident) a multilingual society. Another is that, if Paul were able to speak both Greek and Aramaic, many first-century Jews would also have been able to do so. A third conclusion is the question of whether the commander, who obviously was a Greek speaker (21:37), was also able to speak Aramaic by virtue of his interaction with the crowd (see 21:33–34, 37). A fourth and final

crowd was pleased or affected by this gesture is noticeable in their response—"they became even more quiet" (*μᾶλλον παρέσχον ἡσυχίαν*) (22:2). Linguistic accommodation (in this case, language accommodation) is a clear sign of social convergence; Paul respects his audience, and for that reason, they in turn listen to him. The second evidence is that Paul attempts to establish a social association with his assailants by identifying himself as a native Jew born in Tarsus of Cilicia, raised in this city, and having studied under the rabbi Gamaliel (22:3; cf. 21:39). This social association destabilizes his assailants' accusation about his bringing of Trophimus into the temple. The author's use of three grammatically parallel perfect passive participles—*γεγεννημένος* (having been born), *ἀνατεθραμμένος* (having been brought up), and *πεπαιδευμένος* (having been educated)—to describe Paul's identity highlights this social association. Paul further says that he persecuted the followers of the Way as far as Damascus to punish them and to put them in prison (22:4–5). He asserts that this is a fact that the high priest and all the council of elders can testify to (22:5). Here Paul was not only converging to the crowd, but more specifically, he was associating with the religious leaders who probably were responsible (at least in part) for his arrest. Paul at this point has now converged his language to the crowd and associated himself socially with his assailants. But most importantly, he also has converged to them by appealing to their religious belief; in 22:3, Paul says, "I am . . . being zealous for God as you all are today" (*ἐγώ εἰμι . . . καθὼς πάντες ὑμεῖς ἐστε σήμερον*). His statement is clear: "I am . . . as you all are."

We may now infer what Paul's social motivation and goal (hence, intention) was through these various "convergence" aspects of his testimonial speech. Paul perhaps, in sociolinguistic terms, did not want to project a negative public face in this incident. He still had a glimmer of hope that through his testimonial speech, the Jews would believe and spare him. Paul

conclusion is that language selection in a multilingual society like Palestine serves different purposes and that the use of the appropriate language for the right occasion strengthens social relationships (see 22:2).

accommodates his audience by addressing them in their native Aramaic tongue (21:40; 22:2), exposing his Jewish pedigree (21:39; 22:3–5), and saying, "I am…as you all are today" (22:3). He wants to tell them that they are all members of the same social community; therefore, they should not arrest him. In terms of his interpersonal relation with the crowd, there is absence of superior-subordinate language in the text, and Paul in fact addresses them as "brothers and fathers" (ἄνδρες ἀδελφοὶ καὶ πατέρες) (22:1), which may indicate that the enacted social relationship is one that shows equality of social status. If there were any deferential gesture in Paul's use of the term "fathers," it probably would have been simply used to address the older people in the crowd. Based on this apparent accommodation of language and display of solidarity behavior on Paul's part, it is even plausible to infer further from his testimonial speech that Paul did not distance himself from his assailants during that incident, for he knew already beforehand what was going to happen to him, that is, his appointed time had come (see 22:22). If he had fought back before the arrival of the cohort commander, he could have been killed by the mob and would not have been able to tell his testimonial speech and testimony to them (see 22:1–21). For whatever reasons he had in his mind during that incident, Paul's intention was to tell them about his conversion from a Jewish persecutor of Christ to a Jewish Christian (22:6–21).

4.2 *Mapping out the Structure of the Conversation between Paul and the Cohort Commander in Acts 21:37–40 (Conversation Analysis)*

In between the accusations of Paul's assailants and his response to those accusations, Paul had a short conversation with the cohort commander in Acts 21:37–40. Paul took this chance, which came when he was about to be brought to the barracks (μέλλων τε εἰσάγεσθαι εἰς τὴν παρεμβολὴν), to ask for permission from the commander to speak to the crowd (21:39). Although this conversation between Paul and the commander seems straightforward in the text, that is, Paul asked for permission to speak to the crowd and was granted that permission, it is interesting to note that his request only came at 21:39, when he said, “let me speak to the people” (ἐπίτρεψόν μοι λαλῆσαι πρὸς τὸν λαόν). Nonetheless, his first question to the commander in 21:37—“Could you permit me to say something to you”—should also have been connected to this request. This connection can be explained using conversation analysis, identifying the turn sequences and the structure of the conversation.

There is a total of four turns in the conversation, and each speaker takes an equal number of turns—two turns each for both Paul and the commander. Paul initiates the conversation in 21:37a asking, “Could you permit me to say something to you” (εἰ ἔξεστίν μοι εἰπεῖν τι πρὸς σέ)? This initial turn is composed of a single turn constructional unit (TCU) expressed in the form of an interrogative statement that is embedded as a dependent clause (introduced by the interrogative particle εἰ) in 21:37a. This interrogative statement is followed by a response, the second turn in the conversation, by the commander in 21:37a and 21:38. The response comes in the form of two independent clauses (hence, two TCUs), both of which are insertion sequences that support the commander’s answer to the question as implied in the phrase “but the *commander* was saying” (ὁ δὲ ἔφη) in 21:37b. In other words, both responses—“Do you speak Greek (Ἑλληνιστὶ γινώσκεις)” and “are you not the Egyptian who ‘instigated a revolt’ (ἀναστατώσας) and led out the four thousand Sicarii men into the wilderness (οὐκ ἄρα σὺ εἶ ὁ Αἰγύπτιος ὁ πρὸ τούτων τῶν ἡμερῶν ἀναστατώσας καὶ ἐξαγαγὼν εἰς τὴν ἔρημον τοὺς τετρακισχιλίους ἄνδρας τῶν σικαρίων)”—do not directly answer Paul’s question. Paul’s question concerns a request for permission to speak to the people, but the commander’s reply concerns two other unrelated matters (notice that Paul had to repeat the question again in 21:39—“allow me to speak to the people”).

Nevertheless, Paul answers the commander’s question as he takes his second turn in the conversation with an informative statement (21:39a), “I am a Jew of Tarsus in Cilicia, a citizen of no insignificant city” (ἐγὼ ἄνθρωπος μέν εἰμι Ἰουδαῖος, Ταρσεὺς τῆς Κιλικίας, οὐκ ἀσήμου πόλεως πολίτης), and a request statement expressed in terms of a declarative clause (21:39b), “I beg you" (δέομαι δέ σου), and an imperative clause (21:39c), "allow me to speak to the people" (ἐπίτρεψόν μοι λαλῆσαι πρὸς τὸν λαόν). Paul's answer comprises three TCUs: the informative statement directly responds to the commander's questions in 21:37b and 21:38; and the declarative clause and the imperative clause serve as side sequences (i.e., they directly support what he perhaps was intending to tell the commander—"May I say something to you") to his first turn in 21:37. It is important to note that the imperative clause actually constitutes the main social action that Paul intends to achieve in the conversation. It thus constitutes the first part of the base adjacency pair in the conversation. The second part of the base adjacency pair in the conversation comes at 21:40 when the commander gave Paul permission to speak. What exactly the words of the commander were in granting Paul's request is not stated but implied. This base adjacency pair that is found in 21:39c and 21:40, therefore, serves as the gist or the purpose of this particular social interaction between Paul and the commander.

4.3 *Reconstructing the Context of Situation of Paul's Arrest in the Temple in Acts 21:27–36 (Register Analysis—Systemic Functional Linguistics)*

We have now analyzed the nature of Paul's social relationship with his assailants through his testimonial speech in Acts 21:27—22:5, and we have also looked at the purpose of his conversation with the cohort commander in Acts 21:37–40. In this section, I will attempt to reconstruct the context of situation of Paul's arrest in the temple in Acts 21:27–36 using register analysis. Specifically, I will examine the field, tenor, and mode of the context of situation of Paul's encounter with the crowd in Acts 21:27–36 to say something about what went on during this incident. I begin with the field component, that is, the content, setting, and circumstances of the discourse.

4.3.1 *Field.* The setting of this incident is marked by three sub-settings, all three of which appear to focus on the various activities of the three main participants of the discourse event, that is, "the assembling/gathering crowd" in 21:30b that was instigated by "the Jews from Asia" in 21:27b, the "cohort commander" (ὁ χιλίαρχος), and Paul (ὁ Παῦλος). These three sub-settings altogether tell us of the main circumstances underlying this incident.

The first sub-setting is found in 21:27a: "When the seven days were about to be completed" (ὡς δὲ ἔμελλον αἱ ἑπτὰ ἡμέραι συντελεῖσθαι). This dependent clause introduced by the adverbial conjunction ὡς (when or after) and followed by αἱ ἑπτὰ ἡμέραι tells us about the temporal setting of the event. It also gives us a general overview of the events that immediately happened after Paul completed his purification rites (see 21:26). That the Jews "saw Paul in the temple" (θεασάμενοι αὐτὸν ἐν τῷ ἱερῷ) in 21:27 and that he was eventually dragged out of it (ἐπιλαβόμενοι τοῦ Παύλου εἷλκον αὐτὸν ἔξω τοῦ ἱεροῦ) and the temple doors were shut (ἐκλείσθησαν αἱ θύραι) in 21:30 indicate that the physical setting of this event was in the temple courts. The events that took place involved four participants: the Jews from Asia who stirred up the crowd (οἱ ἀπὸ τῆς Ἀσίας Ἰουδαῖοι . . . συνέχεον πάντα τὸν ὄχλον) in 21:27b and laid hands on Paul (ἐπέβαλον ἐπ' αὐτὸν τὰς χεῖρας) in 21:27c; the whole city that was set in motion (ἐκινήθη ἡ πόλις ὅλη) in 21:30a; the assembling of the crowd that happened (ἐγένετο συνδρομὴ τοῦ λαοῦ) in 21:30b; and the temple doors that were shut (ἐκλείσθησαν αἱ θύραι) in 21:30c. The processes involved comprise two sets of verbal groups, both of which are categorized as "material" processes, that is, they involved physical actions. The first set includes two "active" material processes (i.e., with subject and object)—first, the Jews stirring up (συνέχεον) the crowd; and second, their laying hands (ἐπέβαλον) on Paul. It is important to note that the circumstance involved in the stirring up of the crowd was their shouting (κράζοντες) in 21:28. The second set consists of three "passive" material processes—first, the whole city was set in motion (ἐκινήθη); second, the assembling of the crowd happened (ἐγένετο); and third, the doors were shut (ἐκλείσθησαν).

The second sub-setting is found in 21:31a: "While they were seeking to kill him" (ζητούντων τε αὐτὸν ἀποκτεῖναι). This dependent clause begins with a participial phrase and tells us what took place after the temple doors were shut. There is a change of location from the temple courts to a particular place in the city. During this time, while the assembled crowd was seeking to kill Paul, there were five events that happened, involving two participants—the commander and the crowd. First, "a report went up to the commander" (ἀνέβη φάσις τῷ χιλιάρχῳ) or the commander received a report in 21:31b. Second, "the people stopped beating Paul" (οἱ δὲ ἐπαύσαντο τύπτοντες τὸν Παῦλον) in 21:32. Third, the commander "arrested Paul" (ἐπελάβετο αὐτοῦ) in 21:33a, "ordered him to be bound in two chains" (ἐκέλευσεν δεθῆναι ἁλύσεσι δυσί) in 21:33b, and "was questioning who he was and what he had done" (ἐπυνθάνετο τίς εἴη καὶ τί ἐστιν πεποιηκώς) in 21:33c. Fourth, "some in the crowd were shouting one thing, some another" (ἄλλοι δὲ ἄλλο τι ἐπεφώνουν ἐν τῷ ὄχλῳ) in 21:34a. And fifth, the commander ordered him to be brought into the barracks (ἐκέλευσεν ἄγεσθαι αὐτὸν εἰς τὴν παρεμβολήν) in 21:34b. The processes involved consist of three "active" material processes—a report going up (ἀνέβη) to the commander, the people stopping their beating (ἐπαύσαντο τύπτοντες), and the commander arresting (ἐπελάβετο) Paul, and three verbal processes—the commander ordering (ἐκέλευσεν) the chaining (21:33b) and the bringing of Paul into the barracks (21:34b), the commander questioning (ἐπυνθάνετο) Paul (21:33c), and the crowd shouting (ἐπεφώνουν) one thing to another (21:34a).

The third sub-setting is found in 21:35a: "When he arrived at the stairs" (ὅτε δὲ ἐγένετο ἐπὶ τοὺς ἀναβαθμούς). The location of this third setting moved from a place in the city to a more specific place, that is, at a place near the stairs (τοὺς ἀναβαθμούς), upon the order of the commander (21:34b). This dependent clause is introduced by the adverbial conjunction ὅτε (when), indicating the temporal setting of the incident. There are two events involving two participants that happened in this particular setting. The first event is "the carrying of Paul by the soldiers happened" (συνέβη βαστάζεσθαι αὐτὸν ὑπὸ τῶν στρατιωτῶν) in 21:35b. In this first event, we have an inanimate subject as a participant. However, it is important to note that the implicit subject in this inanimate participant is Paul. Rephrasing this independent clause would read something like this: "what happened was that Paul was carried by the soldiers." And the second event is "the multitude of crowd followed and shouted 'away with him'" (ἠκολούθει γὰρ τὸ πλῆθος τοῦ λαοῦ κράζοντες, Αἶρε αὐτόν) in 21:36. The processes involved in this incident include two material processes, one passive (συνέβη βαστάζεσθαι) and the other active (ἠκολούθει), and a verbal process (κράζοντες).

Grouping together the participants and the corresponding processes associated with them, we can see that the first two main participants (i.e., the crowd and the cohort commander) were responsible for the material processes that were acted on Paul (the Jews laid hands on Paul; the crowd stopped beating Paul; and the commander arrested Paul and bound him in two chains) as well as the verbal processes that were brought up against him (the crowd shouting in stirring up the crowd; the commander questioning who Paul was and what he had done; the crowd shouting various things; the commander ordering Paul to be brought to the barracks; and the crowd shouting to get rid of Paul). The third main participant, Paul, was the victim (i.e., the receiver) of these material and verbal processes.

I now turn to the second component of register analysis, which is the tenor of discourse to determine how these processes were negotiated between these participants.

4.3.2 *Tenor*. With reference to the tenor of discourse, virtually all the finite verbs in the discourse are in the third-person indicative mood form. This is expected, since the account in 22:27–36 is a narrative that is told by the author of Acts. Thus, in order to determine the negotiations of the processes between the participants, we need to examine and interpret these mood forms in the light of what could plausibly have happened in the actual event. Here it is important to set aside the background material in the analysis, which means that only the verbal processes in the discourse need analysis. We can identify three sets of verbal processes in the discourse. They involve the Jews from Asia, the commander, and the crowd; we have already dealt with Paul's interaction with them (see the section above, *Analyzing the*

Social Relationship between Paul and the Crowd in Acts 21:27—22:5), which only came at 21:37.

The first set is embedded within the circumstance of the processes of the stirring up of the crowd (21:27b) and the seizing of Paul (21:27c). As the Jews from Asia were doing these things, they were also calling (κράζοντες) out a message to the crowd (21:28a). The purpose of the message was to "demand for a service" through the use of the second-person plural imperative βοηθεῖτε (come to our aid). Accompanying this purpose were three sets of information (or reasons) these Jews gave to the crowd negotiated in terms of three declarative statements: first, "this is (ἐστιν) the man who preaches to all men everywhere against our people and the law and this place" (21:28b); second, "he brought in (εἰσήγαγεν) Greeks to the temple" (21:28c); and third, "he has defiled (κεκοίνωκεν) this holy place" (21:28d).[50]

The second set is found in 21:33–34 and involves the commander. When the commander came to Paul and took hold of him, he gave an order that Paul (through his soldiers of course) be bound with two chains (21:33b). Subsequently, when the commander was confused about what happened because of the uproar, he gave another order that Paul be brought into the barracks (21:34b). The text indicates that the verb ἐκέλευσεν (he ordered), which is used in both cases, is in the indicative mood, but "to order" of course in the actual event is to demand for goods or services; hence, the indicative is being used as a command. The commander also began to question Paul about his identity and actions (21:33c). Again, the verb form of ἐπυνθάνετο (he was questioning) is in the indicative mood, but "to question" someone in actuality is to demand for information; hence, the speech function is that of asking a question.

50. It is perhaps important to note the use of the perfect tense-form κεκοίνωκεν here. It is possible that the author is highlighting the fact that the bringing of the Greeks into the temple was a defilement of the temple. This fact is supported by the following verse with the use of another perfect tense-form προεωρακότες (had previously seen) in reference to Paul's association with Trophimus the Ephesian (22:29). This could be the main reason for the arrest.

The third set of verbal processes is found in 21:34 and 21:36 and involves the crowd. Some in the crowd were shouting one thing after another (22:34a), such that the commander became confused as to the truth of the matter (δὲ αὐτοῦ γνῶναι τὸ ἀσφαλὲς). Whereas the Jews from Asia in 21:28a called out (κράζοντες) to the crowd to demand for a service, that is, to come to their aid, the crowd here in 22:34a was evidently calling out (ἐπεφώνουν) to bring false accusations against Paul to such a degree that their accusations do not match each other.[51] Nevertheless, the intentions of both the Jews from Asia, and eventually of the crowd, are in one accord: as they followed Paul into the barracks, they were shouting (κράζοντες), "Away with him" (αἶρε αὐτόν) (21:36; cf. 21:31a). The Jews demanded aid from the crowd (21:28a), and together they demanded to get rid of Paul (21:36). The verb αἶρε (to take away) is in the imperative mood.

Analyzing the negotiations that transpired between these three participants, we can observe that the Jews from Asia were actually the ones responsible for the arrest of Paul, as they were the ones who called out for help from the crowd, and they were also involved in the pronouncement of false accusations against Paul and his arrest. Both the crowd and commander were instruments that were used by these Jews in their attempt to get rid of Paul. On the one hand, the crowd gave false accusations and demanded to get rid of Paul. On the other hand, the commander was responsible for the questioning and arrest of Paul.

I now turn to analyze the textual component of the discourse in order to analyze the organization of the message.

4.3.3 *Mode*. With reference to the mode of the discourse, we need to look at the text from the perspective of the author as to how he organized the narrative. Unless the discourse is in a conversational mode, there is no point for us to examine the organization of the discourse in its original (or actual) context of

51. Both ἐπεφώνουν and κράζοντες belong to the semantic sub-domain "Speak, Talk" (see Louw and Nida, *Lexicon*, 1:396–98).

situation. After all, the discourse is a narrative told from the perspective of its author. I have already indicated in my discussion of the field of discourse the three sub-settings of the discourse. From a textual perspective, this is one of the ways to see how the author organizes the general framework of the narrative, that is, by way of three dependent clauses that serve as adjuncts for the processes that introduce the three major participants of the discourse—the Jews from Asia (21:27a) together with the gathered crowd (21:27b), the cohort commander (21:31a), and Paul (21:35). This is also perhaps the way the author wants to highlight the "points of departure" of the passage both to introduce the participants and to indicate the settings of the discourse. Within each of these narratival frameworks, there is what is known as "cohesive chains" that bind the elements in the narrative together.

In 21:27–30, we see a participant chain that begins with the term "crowd" (τὸν ὄχλον) at 21:27, which is subsequently followed by a series of nominal and verbal forms (in Greek, the subject is implied in the verb) that refer to it: "men of Israel" (ἄνδρες Ἰσραηλῖται) in 21:28, "they" (in the verbs προεωρακότες and ἐνόμιζον) in 21:29, and "the people" (τοῦ λαοῦ) in 21:30. We also see a second set of participant chains in the form of nouns as well as pronouns that refer to ὁ Παῦλος (Paul) in 21:29: "him" (αὐτὸν) in 21:27, "the man" (ὁ ἄνθρωπος) in 21:28, and "Paul" (τοῦ Παύλου) in 21:30. There is also a lexical chain that links them together; the noun ἱερόν (temple) is found in all verses, which consequently indicates that the geographical setting of this episode in the narrative was in the temple.

In 21:31–34, the two participant chains that refer to the crowd and Paul continue on in these verses. Reference to the crowd is found in the plural participle "they were seeking" (ζητούντων) in 21:31, in the implied subject in the verb "they stopped" (ἐπαύσαντο) in 21:32, and in the phrase "the crowd" (τῷ ὄχλῳ) in 21:34. Reference to Paul is found in the pronoun αὐτὸν and αὐτοῦ (him) in 21:31, 34 and 21:33, respectively, and in the phrase "Paul" (τὸν Παῦλον) in 21:32. A lexical chain ὁ χιλίαρχος (cohort commander) introducing and linking the new participant is also found in 21:31–33, with an anaphoric pronominal reference "he" (αὐτοῦ) at 21:34 (note the reference to Paul in 21:34 is αὐτὸν).

In 21:35–36, we continue to notice the participant chains that refer to Paul and the crowd. Whereas reference to the crowd is found in the phrases "the crowd" (τοῦ ὄχλου) in 21:35 and "the people" (τοῦ λαοῦ) in 21:36, reference to Paul is found in the pronoun "him" (αὐτὸν) in both verses. It is interesting to note that beginning with 21:37, the participant "crowd" disappears and will not be seen again until 21:40.

There are still other kinds of cohesive ties that can be found in the passage. But this brief analysis of the textual component (mode) of the discourse allows us to see how the author groups the discourse into chunks of information that correspond to both the ideational (field) and interpersonal (tenor) components of the discourse. Together, they tell us much about the context of situation of Paul's arrest in the temple as I have shown in the above discussion.

5. *Conclusion*

My objective in this article from the outset has been to showcase three sociolinguistic approaches that can be used for analyzing texts or discourses in the New Testament. Each of these approaches has their own particular strengths as well as focus in terms of the kinds of aspects or elements in the text that need analysis. Whereas the first approach (social agent focused), as exemplified in my use of social identity theory and communication accommodation theory, can be appositely used in analyzing the social and power relationships among the participants of a discourse, the second approach (text focused), conversation analysis, can best be used for mapping out the structure and organization sequence of texts or discourses that are conversational in nature. The third approach (system network focused), SFL register analysis, is a powerful theory that can be used to get at the context of situation of a text.

With reference to Acts 21:27—22:5, this study has provided many kinds of information that are relevant for the exegesis of the text. These kinds of information include those that tell us about the contextual aspects of the text, such as its social setting, purpose, message, goals, structure, and most importantly, the sociolinguistic context of the incident of Paul's arrest in the temple. It is the aim of this study that future exegetical studies on the texts of the New Testament will consider the use of sociolinguistic theories in order to arrive at a better understanding of the context of a text.

Bibliography

Baird, William. *History of New Testament Research.* 3 vols. Minneapolis: Fortress, 1992–2013.

Black, David A., and David S. Dockery, eds. *Interpreting the New Testament: Essays on Methods and Issues.* Nashville: Broadman & Holman, 2001.

Brown, Gillian, and George Yule. *Discourse Analysis.* Cambridge: Cambridge University Press. 1983.

Bruce, F.F. *The Book of Acts.* NICNT. Revised ed. Grand Rapids: Eerdmans, 1988.

Butler, Christopher S. *Systemic Linguistics: Theory and Applications.* London: Batsford Academic, 1985.

Clermont-Ganneau, C.S. "Discovery of a Tablet from Herod's Temple." *PEQ* 3 (1871) 132–33.

Conzelmann, Hans, and Andreas Lindemann. *Interpreting the New Testament: An Introduction to the Principles and Methods of New Testament Exegesis.* Translated by S.S. Schatzmann. Peabody, MA: Hendrickson, 1988.

Coulthard, Malcolm. *An Introduction to Discourse Analysis.* Harlow, UK: Longman, 1977.

Coupland, Nikolas. "Accommodation at Work." *International Journal of the Sociology of Language* 46 (1984) 49–70.

Drew, Paul. "Conversation Analysis." In *Handbook of Language and Social Interaction*, edited by Kristine L. Fitch and Robert E. Sanders, 71–102. Mahwah, NJ: Lawrence Erlbaum, 2005.

Edwards, Derek. "Discursive Psychology." In *Handbook of Language and Social Interaction*, edited by Kristine L. Fitch and Robert E. Sanders, 257–73. Mahwah, NJ: Lawrence Erlbaum, 2005.

Fairclough, Norman. *Discourse and Social Change*. Malden, MA: Polity, 1993.

Fee, Gordon D. *New Testament Exegesis: A Handbook for Students and Pastors*. Revised ed. Louisville, KY: Westminster John Knox, 1993.

Ferguson, Charles A. “Diglossia,” In *Sociolinguistic Perspectives: Papers on Language in Society by Charles A. Ferguson, 1959–1994*, edited by Thom Huebner, 25–39. New York: Oxford University Press, 1996.

Fishman, Joshua A. “The Relationship between Micro- and Macro-Sociolinguistics in the Study of Who Speaks What Language to Whom and When.” In *Sociolinguistics: Selected Readings*, edited by J.B. Pride and Janet Holmes, 15–32. Harmondsworth: Penguin, 1972.

Giles, Howard, and Nikolas Coupland. *Language: Contexts and Consequences*. Mapping Social Psychology Series. Pacific Grove, CA: Brooks/Cole, 1991.

Giles, Howard, and Richard Street. “Speech Accommodation Theory: A Social Cognitive Approach to Language and Speech Behavior.” In *Social Cognition and Communication*, edited by Michael E. Roloff and Charles R. Berger, 193–226. Beverly Hills: Sage, 1982.

Goodwin, Charles, and Alessandro Duranti. “Rethinking Context: An Introduction.” In *Rethinking Context: Language as an Interactive Phenomenon*, edited by A. Duranti and C. Goodwin, 1–42. Cambridge: Cambridge University Press, 1992.

Green, Joel B., ed. *Hearing the New Testament: Strategies for Interpretation*. 2nd ed. Grand Rapids: Eerdmans, 2010.

Halliday, M.A.K. *Explorations in the Functions of Language*. London: Edward Arnold, 1973.

_______. *An Introduction to Functional Grammar*. 3rd ed. Revised by Christian M.I.M. Matthiessen. London: Edward Arnold, 2004.

_______. *Language and Society, Vol. 10: The Collected Works of M.A.K. Halliday*. Edited by Jonathan L. Webster. London: Continuum, 2009.

_______. *Language as Social Semiotic: The Social Interpretation of Language and Meaning*. London: Edward Arnold, 1978.

Hayes, John H., and Carl R. Holladay. *Biblical Exegesis: A Beginner’s Handbook*. 2nd ed. London: SCM, 1987.

Holmes, Janet. *Introduction to Sociolinguistics*. 3rd ed. Harlow, UK: Pearson & Longman, 2008.

Hudson, Richard. *Sociolinguistics*. 2nd ed. Cambridge: Cambridge University Press, 1996.

Illife, J.H. "The ΘΑΝΑΤΟΣ Inscription from Herod's Temple." *Quarterly of the Department of Antiquities of Palestine* 6 (1936) 1–3.

Kümmel, Werner Georg. *The New Testament: The History of the Investigation of Its Problems*. New Testament Library. Translated by S. McLean Gilmour and H.C. Kee. London: SCM, 1973.

Louw, Johannes P., and Eugene A. Nida. *Greek-English Lexicon of the New Testament: Based on Semantic Domains*. 2 vols. 2nd ed. New York: UBS, 1989.

Malinowski, Bronislaw. "The Problem of Meaning in Primitive Languages." In *The Meaning of Meaning*, by C.K. Ogden and I.A. Richards, 296–336. New York: Harcourt, Brace and World, 1923.

Marshall, I. Howard, ed. *New Testament Interpretation: Essays on Principles and Methods*. Exeter: Paternoster, 1979.

_______. "The Problem of New Testament Exegesis." *JETS* 17.2 (1974) 67–73.

Matthiessen, Christian M.I.M., and Diana Slade. "Analysing Conversation." In *The Sage Handbook of Sociolinguistics*, edited by Ruth Wodak, Barbara Johnstone, and Paul Kerswill, 375–95. Thousand Oaks, CA: Sage Publications, 2011.

McKnight, Scot, and Grant R. Osborne, eds. *The Face of New Testament Studies: A Survey of Recent Research*. Grand Rapids: Baker, 2004.

Ong, Hughson T. "An Evaluation of the Aramaic and Greek Language Criteria in Historical Jesus Research: A Sociolinguistic Study of Mark 14, 32–65." *Filología Neotestamentaria* 45 (2012) 37–55.

_______. "Language Choice in Ancient Palestine." *BAGL* 1 (2012) 63–101.

_______. *The Multilingual Jesus and the Sociolinguistic World of the New Testament*. Linguistic Biblical Studies 12. Leiden: Brill, 2015.

Porter, Stanley E. "Dialect and Register in the Greek of the New Testament: Theory." In *Rethinking Contexts, Rereading Texts: Contributions from the Social Sciences to Biblical Interpretation*, edited by M. Daniel Carroll R., 190–208. JSOTSup 299. Sheffield: Sheffield Academic, 2000.

______. *Idioms of the Greek New Testament*. 2nd ed. Biblical Language: Greek 2. Sheffield: JSOT Press, 1994.

______. "Register in the Greek of the New Testament: Application with Reference to Mark's Gospel." In *Rethinking Contexts, Rereading Texts: Contributions from the Social Sciences to Biblical Interpretation*, edited by M. Daniel Carroll R., 209–29. JSOTSup 299. Sheffield: Sheffield Academic, 2000.

______. "Systemic Functional Linguistics and the Greek Language: The Need for Further Modeling." In *Modeling Biblical Language: Studies in Theory and Practice*, edited by Stanley E. Porter, Gregory P. Fewster, and Christopher D. Land. Linguistic Biblical Studies 13. Leiden: Brill, forthcoming.

______. *Verbal Aspect in the Greek of the New Testament, with Reference to Tense and Mood*. Studies in Biblical Greek 1. New York: Peter Lang, 1989.

Porter, Stanley E., and Jason C. Robinson. *Hermeneutics: An Introduction to Interpretive Theory*. Grand Rapids: Eerdmans, 2011.

Porter, Stanley E., and Kent D. Clarke. "What Is Exegesis? An Analysis of Various Definitions." In *Handbook to Exegesis of the New Testament*, edited by Stanley E. Porter, 3–21. Leiden: Brill, 1997.

Sacks, Harvey. "An Initial Investigation of the Usability of Conversational Data for Doing Sociology." In *Studies in Social Interaction*, edited by D. Sudnow, 31–74. New York: Free Press, 1972.

______. *Lectures on Conversation, Vol. 2*. Edited by Gail Jefferson. Oxford: Blackwell, 1992.

Sacks, Harvey, Emanuel Schegloff, and Gail Jefferson. "A Simplest Systematics for the Organization of Turn-Taking for Conversation." *Language* 50.4 (1974) 696–735.

Shuy, Roger. "A Brief History of American Sociolinguistics." In *The Early Days of Sociolinguistics: Memories and Reflections*, edited by Christina Bratt Paulston and Richard G. Tucker, 11–32. Dallas: Summer Institute of Linguistics, 1997. Reprinted from *Historiographia Linguistica* 17.1 (1990) 183–209.

Sinclair, John, and Malcolm Coulthard. *Towards an Analysis of Discourse*. London: Oxford University Press, 1975.

Tajfel, Henri. *Human Groups and Social Categories: Studies in Social Psychology*. Cambridge: Cambridge University Press, 1981.

______. *Social Identity and Intergroup Relations*. European Studies in Social Psychology. Cambridge: Cambridge University Press, 1982.

Thiselton, Anthony C. *Hermeneutics: An Introduction*. Grand Rapids: Eerdmans, 2009.

______. *The Two Horizons: New Testament Hermeneutics and Philosophical Description with Special Reference to Heidegger, Bultmann, Gadamer, and Wittgenstein*. Grand Rapids: Eerdmans, 1980.

Thompson, Geoff. *Introducing Functional Grammar*. 2nd ed. London: Hodder, 2004.

Wardhaugh, Ronald. *An Introduction to Sociolinguistics*. 5th ed. Oxford: Blackwell, 2005.

[*BAGL* 4 (2015) 85–120]

"Prodding with Prosody": Persuasion and Social Influence through the Lens of Appraisal Theory

James D. Dvorak
Oklahoma Christian University, Edmond, OK, USA

Abstract: This article approaches the topic of persuasion from a social perspective rather than rhetorical or socio-rhetorical. This is because, at heart, persuasion—of others or of self—is ultimately a social action in which values are negotiated. Dvorak argues that to analyze the persuasiveness of a discourse requires a sociolinguistic model, and the model that is best suited for the job is Appraisal Theory, which is built upon the theoretical foundation of Systemic Functional Linguistics. (Article)

Keywords: persuasion, appraisal, evaluation, 1 Corinthians, values, power, discourse analysis.

1. *Introduction*

As the literature bears out, one may engage her- or himself in researching persuasion and social influence in a variety of ways from a variety of perspectives. Common perspectives on the topic come from a broad range of disciplines including, but certainly not limited to, communication, psychology, and neuroscience. The researches from these disciplines have produced a cache of useful information and insights, much of it, perhaps not surprisingly, being focused on the mind and the brain. The major research questions in these areas of inquiry appear to be concerned primarily with (1) how a person's mind processes persuasive messages and (2) what key neurological and physiological reflexes occur in the brain when a person receives messages that the sender(s) intended to be persuasive.

However, my inquiry differs from these researches in that I am more interested in persuasion as a social action and how persuasion is accomplished (or is at least attempted) with language. In this article, I want to address two basic research questions. First, what makes a "persuasive message" *persuasive*? Second, in what way(s) do these messages apply social pressure on people either to adopt a particular point of view or to solidify their adherence to a particular point of view they have already taken up? In what follows, I will address these questions from a sociolinguistic point of view, particularly with a model of appraisal that is firmly nestled in the paradigm of Systemic Functional Linguistics.[1] I focus my investigation on the linguistics of reader or hearer positioning; that is, I analyze text for the discursive features that point to how a person uses language both to take up value positions (i.e., "stances") toward themselves, others, things, ideas, etc., and how a person "prods" others to align with the value position(s) they have adopted and are promoting. I argue that this kind of persuasive prodding is a form of interpersonal meaning that is made through the evaluations or appraisals that one makes and expresses with language.[2] Additionally, I argue that the relative strength of persuasive prodding correlates with the prosodic structure of interpersonal meaning,[3] which adds "a continuous motif or

1. In order to avoid anachronism, I also draw upon, where applicable, the work of social-scientific critics, particularly those that focus on the social and cultural factors that would likely have influenced and constrained social interaction.

2. Following Lemke ("Semantics and Social Values," 39), I presume that people do not use language "simply to organize or to describe (or even create) events and their relations. *Language is also a resource for the creation and maintenance of social relations and value systems.* Every discourse voice, embodied in text, constructs a stance toward itself and other discourse voices. It *evaluates*, explicitly or implicitly, what it has to say and the relation of what it has to say to what *others* do say or may say. Its evaluative orientation includes but is not limited to, certitude of truth value. It can define any value orientation toward what it says and/or toward what others say: appropriateness, usefulness, morality, pleasurability; all the forms of 'rightness' and 'goodness.'" See also Fairclough, *Discourse and Social Change*, 62–100.

3. See Dvorak, "Interpersonal Metafunction," 21–22 (available online at

coloring"[4] that builds over a stretch of text and ultimately reveals the language user's "stance."[5]

My attempt at answering the research questions I have laid out will involve three basic moves. First, I will introduce a working definition of persuasion and will emphasize the point that persuasion is fundamentally social in nature. Then I will sketch the linguistic model that I believe is most suitable for analyzing the persuasiveness of a text. Finally, I will apply the model to 1 Cor 1:26–31 both to demonstrate how the model works and to reveal the linguistic features of persuasion Paul puts to work in order to prod his readers[6] toward unity.

2. *What is Meant by Persuasion?*

From the works of ancient philosophers like Aristotle[7] to those of modern rhetorical theorists such as Perelman and Olbrechts-Tyteca,[8] the vast literature on the topics of rhetoric, argumentation, and, more specifically, persuasion demonstrates that defining persuasion is not without its difficulties. Typically, disagreements arise regarding issues such as determining whether or not intention matters; whether or not someone is actually persuaded and how such can be known; whether or not coercion should count as persuasion; whether or not persuasion requires synchronous linguistic communication; whether or not the nature and type of communication media involved affect persuasion, and if so, the extent of their impact; and the ways and extent to which sociocultural factors come to bear on

http://bit.ly/1Cor1-4); Halliday, "Modes of Meaning," 205; Martin, *English Text*, 11; Martin and White, *Language of Evaluation*, 18–19; Hood, "Persuasive Power of Prosodies," 38.

4. Halliday, "Modes of Meaning," 205; Martin and White, *Language of Evaluation*, 18–19.

5. See Martin and White, *Language of Evaluation*, 163–4.

6. Throughout this paper, I refer to writers and readers; however, the principles presented also apply to speakers and hearers.

7. See, e.g., Aristotle, *Rhet.* 1.2.1 (LCL) for a definition of persuasion. See also his connection of *ethos*, *pathos*, and *logos* to persuasion (1.2.3–7).

8. See, e.g., Perelman and Olbrechts-Tyteca, *New Rhetoric*, XX.

persuasion.[9] Although debate continues over these and related issues, one is still able to distill from the literature a generally agreed upon core description of persuasion. Gass and Seiter state it well:

> . . . persuasion involves one or more persons who are engaged in the activity of creating, reinforcing, modifying, or extinguishing beliefs, attitudes, intentions, motivations, and/or behaviors within the constraints of a given communication context.[10]

This description provides a solid working definition and leaping-off point for the current study, but several presumptions need to be made explicit for us to see the fundamentally social nature of persuasion.

2.1 *Power and Solidarity*

First, every attempt at persuasion among human beings is at once enabled and constrained by two key dimensions of social relations: *power* and *solidarity*.[11] *Power* or, in Martin's terms, *status*[12] describes one's ability to exercise control over and to gain compliance[13] from another with regard to the other's beliefs, attitudes, behaviors, etc.[14] *Power relations* range from equal to unequal,[15] and the basis of one's power derives typically from

9. See Gass and Seiter, *Persuasion, Social Influence, and Compliance Gaining*, 22–33.

10. Gass and Seiter, *Persuasion, Social Influence, and Compliance Gaining*, 34.

11. See Poynton, *Language and Gender*, 76–86; Eggins, *Introduction*, 99–102; Goatly, *Critical Reading and Writing*, 85–86.

12. Martin and Rose, *Genre Relations*, 12.

13. Compliance refers to the act of conforming one's beliefs, attitudes, behaviors, etc., to the wishes or desires of another (see McVann, "Compliance," 33).

14. See Pilch, "Power," 158.

15. See the system network diagram for tenor in Poynton, *Language and Gender*, 77 and Goatly, *Critical Reading and Writing*, 86. Fairclough (*Language and Power*, 26–27) makes an important point about power that is worth noting here: "Power is not in itself bad. On the contrary, the power of people to do things is generally a social good. We need to distinguish between the 'power to' do things and 'power over' other people, though we need to see this binary (and others) in a dialectical way: having power over people

more than one of the following factors: force, authority, status, and expertise.[16] *Force* (physical or otherwise) is related to assertiveness; i.e., "qualities related to boldness, openness, frankness, self-confidence."[17] *Authority* is the "socially recognized and approved ability to control the behavior of others."[18] *Status* refers to the relative social rank of a person "with respect to a socially-desirable object or standing or achievement."[19] *Expertise* "is a matter of the extent to which an individual possesses knowledge or skill."[20]

Solidarity or, in Poynton's scheme, *contact*[21] describes the social distance[22] or strength of relatedness between the members of a group, the measure of which is how strongly they adhere to the group's core values.[23] *Solidarity relations* range from cohesive (i.e., stronger adherence) to discohesive (i.e., weaker

increases power to do things; power to do things is conditional (in some cases at least) on having power over people. But 'power over' is not inherently bad either, as long as it is legitimate; we vote in elections for governments or councils which have various forms of legitimate power over the rest of us, and when we go to a doctor or to a school or university, we recognize that the doctor or teacher has certain legitimate powers over us. Having and exercising power over other people becomes open to critique when it is not legitimate, or when it has bad effects, for instance when it results in unacceptable and unjustifiable damage to people or to social life."

16. Poynton, *Language and Gender*, 76–77.

17. See Reese, "Assertiveness," 10. See also Goatly, *Critical Reading and Writing*, 90–93.

18. Malina, "Authoritarianism," 12.

19. Poynton, *Language and Gender*, 76–77.

20. Poynton, *Language and Gender*, 77.

21. Poynton, *Language and Gender*, 76.

22. See Halliday and Hasan, *Language, Context, and Text*, 57.

23. See Brown and Gilman, "Pronouns of Power and Solidarity," 252–82; Hudson, *Sociolinguistics*, 122. See also Osiek, "Relatedness," 176. The term *value* "describes some general quality and direction in life that human beings are expected to embody in their behavior. A value is a general, normative orientation of action in a social system. It is an emotional anchored commitment to pursue and support certain directions or types of action" (Pilch and Malina, eds., *Handbook of Biblical Social Values*, xv; see also Berger and Luckmann, *Social Construction of Reality*, 93–94 [under "legitimation"] and Anderson and Taylor, *Sociology*, 33).

adherence).[24] These relations wax and wane in correlation with both the amount and the kinds of contact group members have with one another (resulting in varying degrees of familiarity), as well as the "emotional charge" of these relations.[25]

Of course, some configuration of these dimensions is activated in every social interaction, but they are often foregrounded and more obvious in contexts of persuasion. For example, in most societies (if not all), teachers have more power than students because (a) the role of "teacher" has been granted authority in the social system; (b) teachers generally have greater expertise than students; and (c) teachers have achieved higher social status than students, usually by having earned credentials that are valued in the social system. The teacher will utilize this unequal power relationship—especially expertise—to convince her students of this or that point of view. In doing so, she puts the solidarity of the group at some level of risk, depending upon the extent to which it challenges the students' current beliefs and attitudes on the subject matter.

Even in instances where the power distance between participants is negligible, for example between two siblings who are arguing about who is the greatest quarterback in the history of the NFL, part of vying for their individual points of view involves vying for power. This may result in spouting statistics (an expression of expertise), arguing on the basis of prior experience playing football (an expression of status), or perhaps even name calling and other forms of "friendly" berating (expressions of force). Solidarity is still put at risk, and the closer one or the other of these brothers gets to "crossing the line" in any of these three areas, the greater the threat to solidarity.

24. Poynton (*Language and Gender*, 77–78) prefers to measure solidarity in terms of frequency of contact, proliferation, and contraction. The basic idea is that the stronger the relatedness between group members the more meanings those members have available to exchange with one another and the less linguistic "work" it takes to exchange them. See Martin and White, *Language of Evaluation*, 30; Martin, *English Text*, 526, 528–32; Eggins, *Introduction*, 100; Dvorak, "Interpersonal Meaning," 28–30.

25. Martin and Rose, *Genre Relations*, 12.

2.2 *Social Action*

Second, persuasion is a form of social action that is intended to solidify, to modify, or to eliminate one's own or another's values.[26] As mentioned above, people generally bond and create community around some shared set of core values.[27] This occurs as they adopt particular evaluative stances, points of view, or feelings about the world around them.[28] It is in this "investiture of attitude in activity, the resonance of attitude with events and things (abstract or concrete), around which . . . [people] align into communing sympathies of kinship, friendship, collegiality and other of the many kinds of affinity and affiliation."[29] The main social activity involved in generating values-based communities is the construction of axiological paradigms.[30] These are the preferred ways of understanding and evaluating reality from which derive what is normal and deviant, beneficial and harmful, praiseworthy and blameworthy, and so on.[31] In order to win the adherence of the other to the value position(s) being put forward, persuasion plays a pivotal role in naturalizing these models or portraying them as "common sense" (or consensual knowledge) thus making it socially difficult to argue against them.[32]

It is important to remember that solidarity will vary with reference to members' strength of commitment to the group's core values. Thus, one can expect members' value positions to be

26. Fairclough (*Discourse and Social Change*, 63) reminds us that language use is more than a "purely individual activity or mere reflex of situational variables"; it is a means of acting upon the world and upon each other.

27. See Dvorak, "Interpersonal Metafunction," 3; Martin and White, *Language of Evaluation*, 211.

28. See Thompson and Hunston, "Evaluation: An Introduction," 5.

29. Martin and White, *Language of Evaluation*, 211.

30. Axiology is "the study of things with regard to their value dimension" (Neville, *Reconstruction of Thinking*, 12).

31. See Dvorak, "Interpersonal Metafunction," 4. See also White, "Evaluative Semantics," 38.

32. See Dvorak, "Interpersonal Meaning," 42–44; Goatly, *Critical Reading and Writing*, 50, 147–60; Martin, "Reading Positions/Positioning Readers," 22–37.

plotted at varying distances from the "center." Moreover, because people (including the ancients) typically are members of more than one group, and because they regularly come into contact with members of other groups, they are open to pressures to conform to the values of the others and their group(s). This, as a result, creates a more or less agonistic context that has a multi-voiced, or in Bakhtinian terms, heteroglossic backdrop ". . . made up of contradictory opinions, points of view and value judgments . . . pregnant with responses and objections."[33] Each of these voices vies for attention and adherence, so that to some degree every person is involved both in convincing themselves that the value position(s) they have taken up should be maintained and in persuading others to adopt it as well. This is where the social actions of "creating, reinforcing, modifying, or extinguishing" beliefs and behaviors, as emphasized in our working definition above, come into play as part of the constant churn of values negotiation.

2.3 *Semantics of Persuasion*

Finally, persuasion obviously involves communication. Of course, language is not the only means of exchanging persuasive messages, but it is the primary means of doing so.[34] The important point here is not so much *that* language is used to persuade but *how* it is used. Since persuasion is a social action that construes and reconstrues power and solidarity role structures, both of which are tenor variables in register, the semantics of persuasion get expressed as interpersonal meanings.[35] These are the meanings people make "to approve or disapprove; to express belief, opinion, doubt; to include in the social group, or exclude from it; to ask and answer; to express personal feelings; . . ."[36] and so on. These have in common the

33. Bakhtin, *Dialogic Imagination*, 281; Dvorak, "Interpersonal Metafunction, 40–41.

34. See Gass and Seiter, *Persuasion, Social Influence, and Compliance Gaining*, 30–31. See Halliday, *Social Semiotic*, 9.

35. See Halliday, "Functional Basis," 316–17.

36. Halliday, "Functional Basis," 316.

expression of *evaluation*, that is, a person's stance toward the entities or propositions that are at risk in the negotiation of values.[37] It is through evaluation—or appraisal,[38] as I refer to it—that, on the one hand, people confirm and defend their own values and, on the other hand, present those values to others with varying degrees of force for the purpose of generating adherence and solidarity or, perhaps, intentionally to create a separation between "us" and "them" (e.g., 3 John).

2.4 *Summary*

Thus far, I have argued that persuasion is a social action that is both enabled and constrained by the contextual features of power and solidarity; that its purpose is either to solidify or to modify one's own or another's value positions; and that it accomplishes this purpose by positioning oneself or others through the taking up of stance which is, itself, done through expressions of appraisal. I turn now to a brief description of the model to be deployed for the purpose of interpreting the relative persuasiveness of a text.

3. *Model and Method: Appraisal*[39]

Since persuasion occurs through the semantics of evaluation, it seems most appropriate to use a model of discourse analysis[40] that is designed to analyze evaluation, viz. Appraisal Theory.[41]

37. See Thompson and Hunston, "Evaluation: An Introduction," 5; also, Dvorak, "Interpersonal Metafunction," 3.

38. "Appraisal" used here and throughout "refers inclusively to all the evaluative resources of language that a person may use to adopt particular stances or value positions and to negotiate these stances with potential and/or actual respondents" (Dvorak, "Interpersonal Metafunction," 4; see White, "Overview," 2).

39. This section of the paper draws heavily on my dissertation (Dvorak, "Interpersonal Metafunction," 50–104).

40. "Discourse analysis" refers to text-oriented linguistic analysis. See Porter, *Linguistic Analysis*, 133–43.

41. This sort of analysis has traditionally been the work of rhetorical critics, both of the classical (Betz and Kennedy) and "new" (Perelman and

The model describes appraisal as a major discourse semantic resource from which language users make selections in order to make and exchange evaluative meanings. This resource is depicted visually in Fig. 1 as a system network.[42]

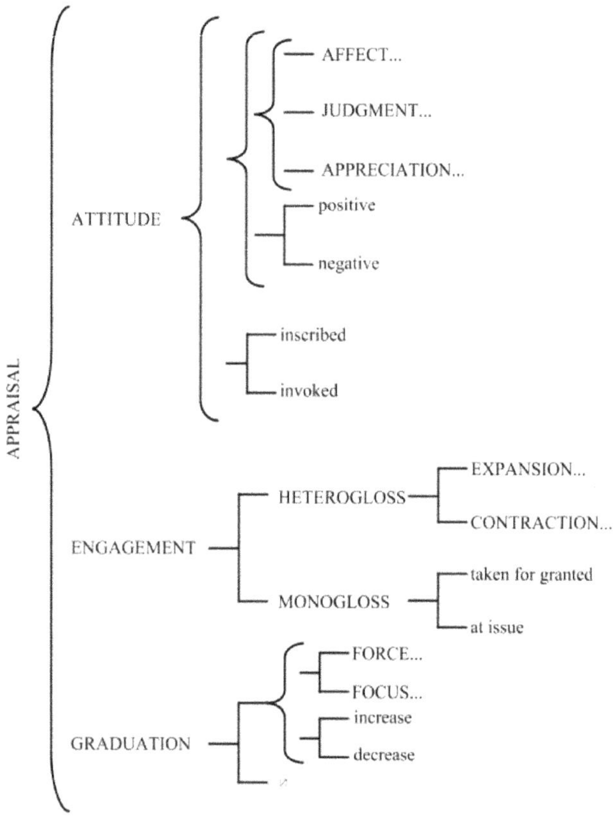

Fig. 1 An Overview of the APPRAISAL System Network[43]

Olbrechts-Tyteca) varieties. Although both of these approaches *may* help interpreters determine *that* a given text is supposed to be persuasive or convincing, in the end they lack the heuristic ability to explain *why* and/or *how* a text is persuasive or convincing (Dvorak, "Interpersonal Metafunction," 50–51).

42. See Dvorak, "Interpersonal Metafunction," 3.

43. Revised and expanded from Dvorak, "Interpersonal Metafunction," 51. See also Martin and White, *Language of Evaluation*, 38, 134, and 154. For

Reading the diagram from left to right, the entry condition of the outermost system, APPRAISAL, is the language user's choice to evaluate someone or something in the context of situation or colloquy. The rounded bracket that opens to the subsystems of ATTITUDE, ENGAGEMENT, and GRADUATION, each of which I define below, indicates that the language user may make selections from any or all of these subsystems in the formulation of her or his evaluation. As more delicate selections are made within each subsystem, the options become binary, which is represented in Fig. 1 by squared brackets. For example, when a language user makes selections from ATTITUDE, she or he has the option of stating those evaluations either explicitly (inscribed) or implicitly (invoked) but not both. More delicate selections may be made from three additional subsystems, AFFECT, JUDGMENT, and APPRECIATION, but these selections are limited in terms of polarity to either positive or negative. Selections from the ENGAGEMENT system are more limited in that the language user must decide whether to assume and portray in the colloquy the existence of other voices/value positions (HETEROGLOSS) or not (MONOGLOSS), and if the former, whether to dialogue with those voices (EXPANSION) or to squelch them (CONTRACTION), but not both.

3.1 *ATTITUDE*

The first of the subsystems of APPRAISAL that is represented in Fig. 1 is ATTITUDE. Broadly speaking, this sub-system describes the resources for expressing the kinds of feelings that have traditionally been discussed under the rubrics of emotion, ethics, and aesthetics.[44] These are the features that language users call upon to encode positive or negative feelings, emotions, and attitudes (including judgments and appreciations) about some entity, proposition, or proposal.[45] Appraisal Theory posits that, interpersonally, selections of ATTITUDE have a rhetorical or

more on system networks, see Porter, *Verbal Aspect*, 7–16.

44. Dvorak, "Interpersonal Metafunction," 52.

45. See Ochs and Schiefflen, "Language Has a Heart," 7–25.

instrumental effect on readers or hearers. Generally speaking, expressions of ATTITUDE function as invitations to or demands upon readers (depending on the power relationship in the situation) to form sympathetic bonds with the writer and the writer's value position. If readers accept this invitation and adopt the same feelings as the writer, then some level of solidarity is generated[46] and persuasion (or convincing) is entailed to some degree. This is referred to as "attitudinal positioning."[47] The model also accounts for both inscribed realizations of affect as well as invoked realizations. The former are those realizations of a more explicit, direct nature such as *ἀγαπῶ τὸν πατέρα* ('I love the Father' [John 15:31]), which directly inscribes the speaker's feeling of love and loyalty toward the Father. The latter are less direct or implied realizations, often expressing the attitude through descriptions of affective behaviors such as *ἱκανὸς δὲ κλαυθμὸς ἐγένετο πάντων* ('But considerable weeping began among them all' [Acts 20:37]), where the weeping that ensued among the Ephesian elders implies a feeling of sadness or sorrow.

3.2 *AFFECT*

ATTITUDE is, itself, comprised of three additional subsystems: AFFECT, JUDGMENT, and APPRECIATION. AFFECT describes the resources for encoding positive or negative feelings as they pertain to people, things, processes, or states of affair. These include:

46. See Dvorak, "Interpersonal Metafunction," 55–56. This rhetorical effect varies slightly depending on two factors. The first factor is related to the source of the attitudinal evaluation. In first-person (authorial) attitudinal evaluations, the writer assumes responsibility for the feeling, and thereby asks the reader to feel the same way. Second-person and third-person (non-authorial) attitudinal evaluations function slightly differently. These locutions make it appear as though the writer merely reports the attitudinal evaluations of others. However, the attributed evaluators function as "surrogate evaluators" for the writer (White, "Attitude/Affect," 6). That is, the writer indicates positive or negative attitudinal appraisals by having some reported source respond to the phenomenon under consideration.

47. See Dvorak, "Interpersonal Metafunction," 5.

- "moods of happy or sad and the possibility of directing these feelings at a Trigger by liking or disliking it"[48]
- psycho-social feelings including fear, anxiety, confidence, and trust relative to a person's world and others with whom they share it[49]
- feelings of achievement and frustration in relation to social activities in which one is actively or passively involved[50]

For example, at Phil. 4:11 Paul writes: ἐγὼ γὰρ ἔμαθον ἐν οἷς εἰμι <u>αὐτάρκης</u> εἶναι ('For I learned to be *content* in whatever circumstances'). This text expresses Paul's feeling of security whether he has plenty or is in need. Not only does it reveal his stance toward trusting in God's provision through the hands of the Philippians in situations of plenty or need, it also nudges the readers to adopt the same trusting attitude as they, themselves, may experience plenty or need.

3.3 *JUDGMENT*

JUDGMENT pertains to the resources with which people positively or negatively appraise behavior in relation to group boundaries and norms. Judgments are of two major types. Judgments of *sanction* generally have to do with veracity (i.e., how truthful someone is) or with propriety (i.e., how ethical someone is), while judgments of *esteem* have to do with normality (i.e., how usual or unusual someone is), with capacity (i.e., how able or capable someone is), or with tenacity (i.e., how resolute or dependable a person is).[51] Hebrews 3:19 provides an illustration of both kinds of judgments. The writer says that the ancients 'were not able to enter [God's rest] on account of unbelief' (οὐκ ἠδυνήθησαν εἰσελθεῖν δι' ἀπιστίαν). 'Unable' (ἠδυνήθησαν) implies a negative judgment of esteem regarding the ancients' capacity to act, and 'unbelief' (ἀπιστίαν), which is given as the reason for their incapacity and which is tied very closely to disobedience in the context, is a negative judgment of sanction with regard to propriety. This "double whammy" makes

48. Martin and White, *Language of Evaluation*, 49.
49. Dvorak, "Interpersonal Metafunction," 62.
50. Dvorak, "Interpersonal Metafunction," 63.
51. See Dvorak, "Interpersonal Metafunction," 65.

absolutely clear that the writer values trust and obedience, and that the Christian community being addressed should adopt and demonstrate those values in their own situation.

3.4 *APPRECIATION*

The third subsystem of ATTITUDE is APPRECIATION, which maps the resources people use to appraise positively or negatively such things as form, appearance, composition, impact, and significance, as well as to assign value or honor to things, ideas, and people. Thus, appreciations revolve around one's reactions to the beauty, orderliness, balance, or detail of things, as well as to their social significance.[52] A clear example of APPRECIATION occurs at 1 Tim 1:15: πιστὸς ὁ λόγος καὶ πάσης ἀποδοχῆς ἄξιος ('This saying is *trustworthy* and *worthy of full acceptance*'). The λόγος ('saying/message') referred to here is twice appreciated positively. Expressing that it is both 'trustworthy' and 'worthy of full acceptance' powerfully indicates the very high value the author ascribes to the text and the value position it promotes, and it nudges readers to appreciate it likewise. Another example occurs at Col 2:5 where expressions of AFFECT and APPRECIATION occur together. Here, Paul expresses feelings of joy (χαίρων) as he considers the orderliness and firmness (τὴν τάξιν καὶ τὸ στερέωμα) of the readers' faith. Χαίρων realizes a selection from AFFECT and both τάξιν and στερέωμα realize selections from APPRECIATION. The latter two terms realize positive appreciation of the readers' faith. The former not only signifies Paul's happy feelings about the orderliness and firmness of the Colossians' faith but also invites them to feel the same way about it and, thus, to be convinced that their faith is legitimate and needs not to be amended by the hollow teachings of others (see Col 2:8).

52. This is important because aesthetic achievements are often used as "weapons of justification and legitimation" for various value positions (cf. Malina, *Christian Origins*, 50).

3.5 *ENGAGEMENT*

The second major piece of the APPRAISAL system alongside ATTITUDE is ENGAGEMENT.[53] The meanings made through choices from this area of semiosis traditionally have been dealt with under the headings of “modality,” “epistemic modality,” and “evidentiality.”[54] The model extends the traditional approach by attending not only to writer certainty, commitment, and knowledge with regard to what is spoken or written about but also to the matter of how the writer or speaker engages and positions her or his own voice vis-à-vis other voices and value positions that are referenced in the text.[55] In other words, this subsystem offers choices for mapping how one presents herself or himself “as recognizing, answering, ignoring, challenging, rejecting, fending off, anticipating, or accommodating actual or potential interlocutors and the value positions they represent.”[56] These actions turn on whether a writer wishes to expand or contract dialogue in relation to the alternative voices comprising the heteroglossic backdrop of the text.

3.5.1 *Dialogic Contraction: Proclamation and Disclamation.* Dialogic *contraction* is accomplished through making either proclamations or disclamations. *Proclamations* are expressed in one of three ways. First, a writer may *concur* with their addressees. These are “formulations which announce the addresser as agreeing with, or having the same knowledge as, some projected dialogic partner.”[57] Second, proclamations may be expressed through the *endorsement* of some externally sourced proposition that the writer construes as being correct,

53. See Dvorak, “Interpersonal Metafunction,” 77–93.

54. See Lyons, *Semantics*, 2:787–849; Palmer, *Mood and Modality*; Chafe, “Evidentiality,” 261–72.

55. See Martin and White, *Language of Evaluation*, 2; White, “Beyond Modality and Hedging,” 259–84; White, “Dialogue and Inter-Subjectivity,” 67–80.

56. Martin and White, *Language of Evaluation*, 2. See Dvorak, “Interpersonal Metafunction,” 5.

57. Martin and White, *Language of Evaluation*, 122.

valid, or undeniable.[58] Third, proclamations may be expressed as *pronouncements*. These are formulations involving "authorial emphases or explicit interventions or interpolations"[59] that intend to overpower any contrary voice.

As an example of dialogic contraction, consider *endorsement*. In these locutions, writers exploit the grammar of reported speech to ground the proposition or proposal in some external source,[60] yet—and this is key—they do not completely dissociate their own voices from those of the external sources. Endorsements often occur in the New Testament as so-called "indirect speech" and some direct quotations. However, direct quotations that are set apart with the introductory formula γέγραπται ('it is written') are typically classed as attributions (discussed below) since in those locutions the writer's own voice is replaced by that of the external voice. An example of endorsement is found at 1 Pet 5:5: πάντες δὲ ἀλλήλοις τὴν ταπεινοφροσύνην ἐγκομβώσασθε, ὅτι [ʽO] θεὸς ὑπερηφάνοις ἀντιτάσσεται, ταπεινοῖς δὲ δίδωσιν χάριν ('Now all of you clothe yourselves with humility toward one another, for *God opposes the proud, but gives grace to the humble*'). In this instance, Peter quotes a text from Prov 3:34 LXX, but it is portrayed as his own voice and not explicitly as the voice of God or tradition.

As mentioned, writers may also contract dialogue by means of *disclamation*.[61] This happens when a language user invokes an alternative point of view only to explicitly reject, replace, or show it to be unsustainable.[62] There are two ways to do this: one may outright *deny* an alternative value position or one may *counter* it with another.[63] Expressions of countering are fairly common in the New Testament. One example is found at 1 Cor

58. Martin and White, *Language of Evaluation*, 126. See Dvorak, "Interpersonal Metafunction," 79.

59. Martin and White, *Language of Evaluation*, 127. See Dvorak, "Interpersonal Metafunction," 81–82.

60. See Martin and White, *Language of Evaluation*, 126.

61. See Dvorak, "Interpersonal Metafunction," 82–84.

62. Dvorak, "Interpersonal Metafunction," 82.

63. See Dvorak, "Interpersonal Metafunction," 83–84.

3:6, where Paul states that he planted the gospel and Apollos watered it, but lest the readers think on the basis of these actions that Paul or Apollos are anything more than mere servants of God, Paul counters with 'but God gave the increase' (ἀλλ' ὁ θεὸς αὔξανεν).

3.5.2 *Dialogic Expansion: Consideration and Attribution.* The alternative to dialogic contraction is dialogic *expansion*, which actively creates and often leaves open semiotic "space" for other points of view. There are two ways to expand dialogue in text: by *consideration*[64] or by *attribution*. Considerations are commonly realized by expository or open questions, verbal mood, modal adjuncts, and certain mental process projections.[65] *Attributions*, like endorsements, make reference to some external source. However, whereas in endorsements writers adopt reported speech as their own, in attribution they let the sourced texts speak for themselves to comment on the proposition or proposal at issue.

Attribution is common in the New Testament, often expressed through direct quotations where the introductory formula 'it is written' is used. For example, at Galatians 3:10 Paul asserts, ὅσοι γὰρ ἐξ ἔργων νόμου εἰσίν, ὑπὸ κατάραν εἰσίν ('For those who rely on works of the law are under a curse'). Immediately following this proclamation, he adds, γέγραπται γὰρ ὅτι Ἐπικατάρατος πᾶς ὃς οὐκ ἐμμένει πᾶσιν τοῖς γεγραμμένοις ἐν τῷ βιβλίῳ τοῦ νόμου τοῦ ποιῆσαι αὐτά ('For it is written, "Everyone who does not carefully observe everything written in the book of the Law in order to do these things is cursed"'). Paul, thus, garners support for his assertion from the voice of the Torah itself. This is rhetorically powerful because it positions any alternative point of

64. Martin and White call this "entertain(ment)," as did I in my dissertation (see Dvorak, "Interpersonal Metafunction," 85–87). I have since changed the term to "consideration" in order to communicate that the alternative position is up for consideration in the colloquy.

65. See Martin and White, *Language of Evaluation*, 104–45; Dvorak, "Interpersonal Metafunction," 85.

view as standing opposed not necessarily to Paul but to scripture, tradition, and the teachings of God.[66]

3.6 *GRADUATION*

Finally, the third major subsystem of APPRAISAL is GRADUATION,[67] which traditionally has been discussed under such headings as "intensification," "vague language," and "hedging."[68] Resources in this system allow language users to grade or scale meanings made from the other systems. As Martin and White note,

> . . . a defining property of all attitudinal meanings is their gradability. It is a general property of values of affect, judgment, and appreciation that they construe greater or lesser degrees of positivity or negativity. . . . Gradability is also generally a feature of the engagement system [where meaning scales] more broadly for the degree of the [writer's] intensity or the degree of investment in the utterance.[69]

Although the model of GRADUATION is quite delicate, it will suffice to point out its two major options: (1) sharpening or blurring focus or (2) increasing or decreasing force. Focus allows for scaling things in terms of prototypicality, as in, for example, Paul's address of Timothy as his 'true/genuine son in the faith' (<u>γνησίῳ</u> τέκνῳ ἐν πίστει) at 1 Tim 1:2. Rhetorically, sharpening focus indicates that a writer is maximally invested in the value position being advanced, while softening focus indicates that a writer is less than fully invested in the value position.[70]

Force describes the resources for up-scaling or down-scaling the intensity of propositions or proposals. Increased force construes a writer as highly committed to the value position being advanced as well as strongly attempting to align readers to

66. See Lemke, *Textual Politics*, 49–57, on the function of intertextual thematic formations.

67. See Dvorak, "Interpersonal Metafunction," 84–104.

68. See Labov, "Intensity," 43–70; Channell, *Vague Language*, 1–22; and Lakoff, "Hedges," 183–228.

69. Martin and White, *Language of Evaluation*, 135–36.

70. Dvorak, "Interpersonal Metafunction," 95.

that value position.[71] Alternatively, downscaling force tends to construe a writer as less than fully committed to a value position.[72] The scaling force gets realized in quite a number of ways, but common expressions in the New Testament include repetition, the "piling up" of semantically related words, and the "piling up" of attitude (e.g., κλαύσετε καὶ θρηνήσετε ὑμεῖς ['You will weep and you will wail' (John 16:20)]); the use of adverbial or adjectival modifiers of scale (e.g., οἱ μαθηταὶ ἐξεπλήσσοντο σφόδρα ['The disciples were exceedingly perplexed' (Matt 19:25)]); and the use of lexical items that are infused with greater or lesser degrees of force (compare, e.g., φόβος [pertaining to being afraid] with ἔκφοβος [pertaining to being terrified]).[73]

3.7 *Prosody*

Having outlined the basic resources of the APPRAISAL system, a word needs to be said about how Appraisal Theory articulates prosody. So far what has been described is the system of APPRAISAL and its primary subsystems, which emphasizes the notion that language is a vast system of networks that comprise meaning potential,[74] and that specific meanings are made when language users make selections from these networks. However, Systemic Functional Linguistics puts forward a structural perspective that is complementary to this systemic perspective. The structural perspective "foregrounds the inherent temporality of semiotic processes—they unfold through time, and phases of this process enter into interdependent relations with one another by way of signaling the meanings that are being made" via selections from the system.[75] Pike is usually credited as the first

71. Dvorak, "Interpersonal Metafunction," 95.

72. Dvorak, "Interpersonal Metafunction," 96.

73. On φόβος see LN 25.251 and on ἔκφοβος see LN 25.256.

74. Meaning potential is defined in terms of culture, not in terms of the mind as in the Chomskyan notion of competence. See Halliday, *Explorations in the Functions of Language*, 52.

75. Martin and White, *Language of Evaluation*, 17.

linguist to acknowledge different kinds of text structuring principles when he noted the following:

> Within tagmemic theory there is an assertion that at least three perspectives are utilized by Homo sapiens. On the one hand, he often acts as if he were cutting up sequences into chunks—into segments or *particles* . . . On the other hand, he often senses things are somehow flowing together as ripples on the tide, merging into one another in the form of a hierarchy of little *waves* of experience on still bigger waves. These two perspectives, in turn, are supplemented by a third—the concept of *field* in which intersecting properties of experience cluster into bundles of simultaneous characteristics which together make up the patterns of his experience.[76]

Halliday and his followers extend this notion by associating kinds of structure with kinds of meaning. Using Martin's terms, ideational or presentational[77] meaning is configured segmentally into a *particulate structure* typically consisting of a nucleus (i.e., a Process and Medium), margin (i.e., Agent), and periphery (i.e., circumstances) (Fig. 2).

οὗτος He	προσκαλεσάμενος Βαρναβᾶν καὶ Σαῦλον having summoned Barnabas and Saul	ἐπεζήτησεν sought	ἀκοῦσαι τὸν λόγον τοῦ θεοῦ to hear the word of God
Margin (Agent)	Periphery (Circumstance Role)	Nucleus (Process)	Periphery (Circumstance Role)

Fig. 2 Example of Particulate Structure (Acts 13:7)

Textual or organizational[78] meaning, according to Martin, exhibits *periodic structure* which is configured in "waves of information"[79] that establish "peaks of prominence"[80] in the clause. In Hellenistic Greek, this information is organized by

76. Pike, *Linguistic Concepts*, 12–13. See also Martin and White, *Language of Evaluation*, 17–18.

77. "Presentational meaning" comes from Lemke, *Textual Politics*, 41.

78. "Organizational meaning" comes from Lemke, *Textual Politics*, 41.

79. Martin and White, *Language of Evaluation*, 19.

80. Martin, "Text and Clause," 26.

position in the clause, where the first position, the Prime, is used to highlight who or what the clause is about, and the remainder of the clause, the Subsequent, is used to develop the Prime (Fig. 3).[81]

ὁ φιλοπρωτεύων αὐτῶν Διοτρέφης The one who loves to be first among them, Diotrephes,	οὐκ (does) not	ἐπιδέχεται receive	ἡμᾶς us
Prime	Subsequent		

Fig. 3 Example of Prime and Subsequent Analysis (3 John 9)

Most important for the current study is the characterization of interpersonal or orientational[82] meaning as *prosodic structure*.[83] The notion of prosody stems from phonology, where prosody describes how tone rises and falls in a continuous movement throughout an entire tone group as it unfolds.[84] Halliday perceived an analogous connection to interpersonal/orientational semantics:

> The interpersonal component of meaning is the speaker's ongoing intrusion into the speech situation. It is his perspective on the exchange, his assigning and acting out of speech roles. Interpersonal meanings cannot be easily expressed as configurations of discrete elements [as with ideational meanings] . . . The essence of the meaning potential of this part of the semantic system is that most of the options are associated with the action of meaning as a whole . . . this interpersonal meaning . . . is strung throughout the clause as a continuous motif or coloring . . . the effect is cumulative . . . we shall refer to this type of realization as "prosodic," since the meaning is distributed like a prosody through a continuous stretch of discourse.[85]

There are three types of prosodic realization. The first is *saturation*, which is generated most commonly in the New Testament when a particular choice of ATTITUDE manifests

81. See now Dvorak, "Thematization," 20 and Dvorak and Walton, "Clause as Message," 42–45.

82. "Orientational meaning" is from Lemke, *Textual Politics*, 41.

83. Martin, "Text and Clause," 10.

84. Martin, "Text and Clause," 10.

85. Halliday, "Modes of Meaning," 206.

itself wherever it can at clause level or beyond. For example, at Acts 13:10, when Paul, filled with the Holy Spirit and having just learned that Elymas was trying to divert the proconsul from the faith, unleashes a severely negative judgment of Elymas all in a lengthy address formula: Ὦ πλήρης παντὸς δόλου καὶ πάσης ῥᾳδιουργίας, υἱὲ διαβόλου, ἐχθρὲ πάσης δικαιοσύνης ('O son of the devil who is full of every kind of deceit and all wickedness, enemy of every righteous thing').[86] What's more, this chain of negative judgment is followed by the leading question, οὐ παύσῃ διαστρέφων τὰς ὁδοὺς τοῦ κυρίου τὰς εὐθείας; ('will you not cease making crooked the straight paths of the Lord?'), which creates a *concurrence* in the text on the point that Elymas will, indeed, *not* stop twisting the paths of the Lord—a token of negative judgment. This stretch of text is clearly saturated with negative judgment and it generates a negative prosody that reverberates to the reader and positions her or him to join in the negative judgment of Elymas.

A second kind of prosodic realization is *intensification*. This type of prosody results from selections from the system of GRADUATION that amplify force. As Martin and White put it, this kind of prosody "creates a bigger splash which reverberates through the surrounding discourse."[87] For example, at Matt 2:10 when the *magoi* saw that the star they were following came to rest over the place where Jesus was, Matthew writes that they ἐχάρησαν χαρὰν μεγάλην σφόδρα ('they rejoiced exceedingly a great joy'). Here the uses of the verb χαίρω and cognate noun χαρά as well as the two modifiers that up-scale force, μεγάλη and σφόδρα, generate an intense positive prosody that radiates through the surrounding discourse and outward to the reader positioning her or him to join in the same joyful response.

The third kind of prosodic realization is *domination*. As the label suggests, this kind of prosody is associated with "meanings that have other meanings under their scope."[88] Realizations of this kind of prosody occur in clause complexes where the

86. See Dvorak, "Positioning Readers with Perspective."
87. Martin and White, *Language of Evaluation*, 20.
88. Martin and White, *Language of Evaluation*, 20.

dominant clause somehow "colors" (e.g., modalization) the content of the dependent clause or, perhaps more common in the New Testament, where Adjuncts (e.g., adverbial participle clauses) color the proposition or proposal of the main process of the clause. For example, at Matt 1:19, Matthew records, Ἰωσὴφ δὲ ὁ ἀνὴρ αὐτῆς, δίκαιος ὢν καὶ μὴ θέλων αὐτὴν δειγματίσαι, ἐβουλήθη λάθρᾳ ἀπολῦσαι αὐτήν ('Now, her husband Joseph, *being just and not wanting to publicly disgrace her*, wished to divorce her privately'). In this instance, Matthew's editorial comment 'being just and not wanting to disgrace her' puts a positive "spin" on his desire to divorce Mary. This is an important move in light of the fact that Matthew generally portrays divorce negatively (cf. Matt 5 and 19).[89] Here, however, readers are positioned to view Joseph and his inclination to divorce Mary as at least merciful if not even honorable.

3.8 *Summary*

Although this section has provided only a brief description of the model, it should be enough to provide a sense of its utility. Essentially, the model of appraisal presented above offers a framework for analyzing the persuasive intent of a text. This is based on the premise that persuasion is concerned with positioning others to adopt certain value positions and to eschew others, and that appraisal or evaluation is a key means of accomplishing this kind of reader positioning. Positive or negative expressions of ATTITUDE (i.e., AFFECT, JUDGMENT, and APPRECIATION) reverberate prosodically through portions of text sometimes inviting and sometimes invoking readers to adopt the same feeling and the perspective on the person or topic at hand that such a feeling requires. Additionally, persuaders, by making selections from the ENGAGEMENT system, can utilize various means of expanding or contracting dialogue with alternative value positions. In this way, they can potentially cause a shift in the readers' perspective with regard to those alternative points of view, assuming a compliant reading or

89. See Keener, *Matthew*, 189–92 and 462–72.

hearing. Further, language users can call upon the system of GRADUATION to manage both FORCE and FOCUS such that certain points of view might be foregrounded and others backgrounded as values are negotiated. In short, the model provides a way for discourse analysts to identify what value positions are at stake in a given colloquy and how a writer positions her or his intended audience to adopt the ones that she or he thinks should be adopted.

In the final section of this paper, I will apply the model to 1 Cor 1:26–31, in which I will highlight examples of both ATTITUDE and ENGAGEMENT that Paul employs for persuasive purposes. I will also draw attention to realizations of GRADUATION where they appear to contribute significantly to the semantics of the unit of text under discussion.

4. *The Model Applied: 1 Corinthians 1:26–31*

David deSilva rightly observes that "an especially critical issue for Paul in the Corinthian correspondence is detaching the believers there from their tendency to evaluate a person's worth by the values of the Greco-Roman culture in which they lived."[90] Having heard the report of the envy-driven conflict among them (cf. 1:11), Paul set out to convince (again) the Corinthian Christians that what they were doing was inappropriate in the ἐκκλησία τοῦ θεοῦ. This message is no more apparent than in 1 Cor 1:26–31. Prior to this text, Paul has quite ably argued (1) that judging by the world's standards destroys solidarity/unity among the believers (wholeness is the value put at risk), and (2) that Jesus' death was actually God's way of rendering the world's value system obsolete and void of any power (cf. 1:10–25). In 1:26–31, Paul makes a strong move to bring this point home to the readers. In what follows, I will highlight a number of key persuasive features using the model described above. As will be pointed out, Paul's selections from the systems of ATTITUDE and ENGAGEMENT play a significant role in his

90. deSilva, *Honor*, 74–75.

attempt at persuading the readers to think, believe, and act in a way Paul believes is consonant with the values taught in scripture and lived out by Jesus Christ.

4.1 *Attitudinal Analysis*[91]

The unit begins with a command issued to the readers to consider (βλέπετε) their own station in life (κλῆσις).[92] Immediately following this command, Paul, apparently applies the world's standards to the readers (note *κατὰ σάρκα* ['according to the flesh']), supplies the vision of themselves they are to see: 'many are not wise' (*οὐ πολλοὶ σοφοί*), 'many are not influential' (*οὐ πολλοὶ δυνατοί*), and 'many are not of high status' (*οὐ πολλοὶ εὐγενεῖς*). A few observations are in order.[93] First, the three appraisals are parallel in clause structure, and the adjectives Paul uses all overlap in the semantic domain of social status (cf. LN domain 87). Second, in each clause the negative particle *οὐ* occupies the prime, emphatic position, which realizes a selection from GRADUATION so as to signal prominently negative appraisal. Third, each appraisal is a negative *appreciation* rather than negative judgment. That is, Paul is not here judging the readers' behavior but their social status or worth in society as the world would see them. Taken all together, these features generate a negative prosody both by saturation and by intensification, with the result that the text packs a relatively powerful interpersonal/orientational semiotic punch. The point is to position the readers to conclude that if they were to judge themselves by the world's standards, as they, apparently, are doing to others, they would find they, themselves, are not socially extraordinary in any way. There is, thus, no foundation for boasting (v. 29).

91. In this section, I use a number of notations that need explanation: "t" stands for token, which identifies invoked or implied realizations of attitude; –ve stands for negative; +ve stands for positive.

92. It is not likely that κλῆσις bears the sense of "(divine) calling" here (LN domain 33). It is more likely to mean "station in life" here (LN domain 87), since the series of adjectives with which it collocates are from LN 87 (i.e., σοφοί, δυνατοί, and εὐγενεῖς).

93. These are from Dvorak, "Interpersonal Metafunction," 147–48.

But at v. 27, things change. Paul continues to make selections from APPRECIATION; however, it is no longer Paul who appraises but God, and his appraisals are betokened by his actions, which are presented in a series of three cause-condition[94] clause complexes:

(1) ἀλλὰ τὰ μωρὰ τοῦ κόσμου ἐξελέξατο ὁ θεός,
ἵνα καταισχύνῃ τοὺς σοφούς

But God chose the foolish of the world
in order to shame the wise

(2) καὶ τὰ ἀσθενῆ τοῦ κόσμου ἐξελέξατο ὁ θεός,
ἵνα καταισχύνῃ τὰ ἰσχυρά

and God chose the non-influential of the world,
in order to shame the influential

(3) καὶ τὰ ἀγενῆ τοῦ κόσμου καὶ τὰ ἐξουθενημένα ἐξελέξατο ὁ θεός, τὰ μὴ ὄντα, ἵνα τὰ ὄντα καταργήσῃ

and God chose the insignificant of the world and the despised, the nobodies, in order to render powerless the somebodies.

This threefold structure corresponds to Paul's three evaluations in v. 26;[95] however, here the prosody is not solely negative but alternates between positive and negative. In each of the main clauses, the desiderative/volitional process ἐξελέξατο ('he chose') operates as a token of God's positive appreciation toward the μωρὰ ('foolish'), ἀσθενῆ ('non-influential'), and ἀγενῆ ('insignificant') respectively.[96] By choosing those who inhabit

94. See Halliday and Matthiessen, *Introduction to Functional Grammar*, 418; Reed, "Discourse Analysis," 206–8.

95. The correspondence is not exact. In this set of clause complexes, the final complex varies slightly in length, lexical selection, and scope (though it has the same basic structure). Whereas the previous two clauses have single complements (τὰ μωρὰ and τὰ ἀσθενῆ respectively), this clause contains a double complement, the second of which is a frontgrounded substantival perfect passive participle (τὰ ἀγενῆ and τὰ ἐξουθενημένα). Moreover, the second complement is further defined by an additional substantival participle (τὰ μὴ ὄντα). For these reasons, the third complex should be seen as prominent. See OpenText.org for the clause and word group structures.

96. See LN 30.92. This connects back to εὐδόκησεν in v. 21, which shares the same semantic domain (see LN 30.97).

these social categories,[97] God bestows honor upon them and thereby demon-strates that he positively values them (t, +ve APPRECIATION: valuation). However, that God chooses the foolish, non-influential, and insignificant for the purpose of (ἵνα) shaming the wise and influential and rendering powerless the "somebodies" signifies his negative valuation of those inhabiting these latter categories and, by extension, the ideology by which they operate (t, −ve APPRECIATION: valuation).[98] This is represented by the processes καταισχύνῃ ('he would shame') and καταργήσῃ ('he would destroy'). Being shamed is clearly a negative action in the sociocultural context. It is the social process of status degradation in which one's honor is stripped resulting in being seen as "less than valuable" by others.[99] Further, the sense of καταργήσῃ is constrained by virtue of its collocation with καταισχύνῃ; here it signifies taking away the power/status and influence of the "somebodies."

At v. 29 there is a marked shift from appreciation to judgment, which indicates that Paul now invokes the theme of reversal to appraise a behavior.[100] This clause portrays the reason why God exalted the humble and humbled the exalted: 'so that all humanity should not boast in the presence of God' (ὅπως μὴ καυχήσηται πᾶσα σὰρξ ἐνώπιον τοῦ θεοῦ). In light of the actions of God described in vv. 27–28,[101] 'should not boast' speaks to the impropriety of staking a claim to honor on the basis of one's own

97. Although each epithet is neuter plural (τὰ μωρὰ, τὰ ἀσθενῆ, τὰ ἀγενῆ, τὰ ἐξουθενημένα, and τὰ μὴ ὄντα), they each refer to social categories and, thus, may be thought of personally. See Theissen, "Social Stratification," 70–72; Garland, *1 Corinthians*, 76; Engberg-Pedersen, "The Gospel and Social Practice," 562; Tucker, *You Belong to Christ*, 173–76.

98. On glossing τὰ ὄντα as "somebodies" (and τὰ μὴ ὄντα as "nobodies"), see Thiselton, *First Corinthians*, 185 (though he uses "somethings" and "nothings").

99. See deSilva, *Honor*, 25; Malina and Neyrey, "Honor and Shame in Luke–Acts," 45.

100. Tucker rightly says the ὅπως "encompasses the three previous ἵνα clauses" (*You Belong to Christ*, 175) and, thus, states the greater overall purpose of the three previous cause-condition complexes.

101. See deSilva, "Honor Discourse," 67.

achievements or of using the benefactions from God for self-aggrandizing purposes (− JUDGMENT: propriety). The clause 'the one who boasts is to boast in the Lord' (v. 31), which forms something of an inclusio with v. 29, speaks to the propriety of boasting but only 'in the Lord' (+ JUDGMENT: propriety), so as to give 'the Lord' due honor for his beneficence. Sandwiched between these verses is a poignant explanation as to why it is the Lord and not any human that deserves honor: 'it is by him you are in Christ Jesus' (v. 30). The readers, who earlier in this unit were appraised as less than remarkable, are now re-appraised positively but only because they are 'in Christ' (t, + APPRECIATION: valuation) and they are so only because God's election of the despised and unworthy made it possible.

4.2 *Engagement Analysis*

In terms of ENGAGEMENT, this unit is largely dialogically contractive due to the use of a number of disclamations. These are realized as denials in each of the three paratactic content clauses in v. 26 and are signaled by the negative particle οὐ. In the first clause, Paul rejects the view that 'many were wise according to the flesh'; in the second he rejects the view that 'many were influential'; and in the third he rejects the view that 'many were of high status.' These denials potentially put writer-reader solidarity at risk since they reject positive assessments of the readers' social status. However, ἀλλά signals to the readers that Paul is about to offer some kind of counter proposition. To do so, Paul utilizes antonymy to pair each of the denials with a corresponding counter in vv. 27–28 (σοφοί : μωρά :: δυνατοί : ἀσθενῆ :: εὐγενεῖς : ἀγενῆ). Each counter realigns the readers by supplanting the negative propositions with positive ones.

DENY	COUNTER-EXPECTANCY	COUNTER
οὐ πολλοί σοφοὶ		τὰ μωρὰ . . . ἐξελέξατο ὁ θεός
οὐ πολλοὶ δυνατοί	ἀλλὰ	τὰ ἀσθενῆ . . . ἐξελέξατο ὁ θεός
οὐ πολλοὶ εὐγενεῖς		τὰ ἀγενῆ . . . ἐξελέξατο ὁ θεός

Fig. 4 Deny–Counter Counterexpectancies

The final clause of the unit, 'so that—just as it is written—The one who boasts is to boast in the Lord' is important. Paul quotes Jer 9:22–23 LXX, introducing it with the formula 'it is written,' thereby signaling an attribution. Thus, Paul squelches his own voice and allows the voice of scripture/tradition/God to comment on the matter. That voice monoglossically pronounces that all boasting is excluded, except boasting "in the Lord." This puts the readers in the position of either compliantly taking up the same point of view or resisting scripture, tradition, and/or God.

5. *Summary and Conclusion*

Even in just this brief analysis of a relatively short stretch of text, the model of appraisal has pointed out a number of features that are significant in Paul's attempt to persuade those seemingly powerful among his putative readers to stop judging their brothers and sisters by the standards of the world. First, the attitudinal analysis of v. 26 shows that those among the Corinthian believers who were making a claim to status/power by judging others in the assembly by the world's measuring stick would, themselves, not be able to live up to those standards. By those standards, they, too, would be judged "not wise," "not influential," and "not of high status." Assuming a compliant reading, the negative prosody generated through these three clauses would in the very least gain the attention of these people by challenging their honor.

A second feature identified by the attitudinal analysis is the alternation between positive and negative judgments in v. 27. It is significant that these judgments, as Paul portrays them, do not originate with Paul but with God, as is betokened by God's divine act of choosing. Yet, *that* God chose is *not* the most important point in this text; rather, it is *who* God chose that imbues this text with significant interpersonal/orientational meaning. The foolish, non-influential, and insignificant—those who are social "nobodies" according to the standards of the world (which, as Paul just pointed out, would also include those among the readers who are inappropriately judging their brothers and sisters)—are through God's choosing of them worthy of and invested with honor. What is more, God chose those inhabiting these social categories for the purpose of shaming those whom the world would appraise as wise, influential, and noble—as "somebodies." This means that God has undone the way the world typically measures and grants honor (see 1:18–25). Paul points out that the standards of the world no longer hold sway for those who are in Christ, and those who are in Christ are there solely by God's doing (v. 30). Therefore, all human boasting is powerless and worthless. Those among the readers who claimed expertise in categorizing others and exercised the power to do so no longer have any foundation on which to stand. They are powerless, just like the standards they use to judge others. If the readers agree with God's appraisals (as Paul portrays them), this would go a long way toward persuading them to change their beliefs and behaviors to something that aligns more closely with the core values of the ἐκκλησία, the assembly of Jesus followers.

Finally, the engagement analysis above pointed out the basic rhetorical structure of Paul's argument. In v. 26 he denies that any of the readers were of any significant level of social status, which would potentially put solidarity with the readers at risk. However, he counters these denials with solidarity building proclamations that God chose people of low status—just like them—to be his people. This leads to the monoglossic statement that boasting is inappropriate, since it was by God's doing through the cross of Christ that the readers are in Christ. This is followed by the quotation from scripture (once again God's/tradition's voice, not Paul's) that the one who boasts should boast in the Lord. The use of denial-counter and monoglossic categorical statements virtually squelches all other value positions and points of view. All that is allowed, in the text at least, is the value positions that (a) human standards are supplanted by God's standards; (b) judging fellow believers by the world's standards is inappropriate for those in Christ; and (c) boasting in human accomplishment is inappropriate for those in Christ.

In the end, the core values of those who are part of the ἐκκλησία τοῦ θεοῦ that become evident in this text include: God's standards of honor trump those of the world; boasting in the Lord is the only appropriate kind of boasting for believers; it is only by God's gracious beneficence that believers gain life in Christ. These are the things regarding which Paul wants to convince his readers.

Bibliography

Anderson, Margaret L., and Howard F. Taylor. *Sociology: The Essentials*. 7th ed. Belmont, CA: Wadsworth Cengage, 2013.

Bakhtin, Mikhail M. *The Dialogic Imagination*. Edited by Michael Holquist. Translated by Caryl Emerson and Michael Holquist. Austin: University of Texas Press, 1981.

Berger, Peter L., and Thomas Luckmann. *The Social Construction of Reality: A Treatise in the Sociology of Knowledge*. Garden City, NY: Doubleday, 1966. Reprint. New York: Anchor, 1967.

Brown, R., and A. Gilman. "Pronouns of Power and Solidarity." In *Language and Social Context*, edited by Pier Paolo Giglioli, 252–82. Harmondsworth: Penguin, 1972.

Chafe, Wallace L. "Evidentiality in English Conversation and Academic Writing." In *Evidentiality: The Linguistic Coding of Epistemology*, edited by W.L. Chafe and J. Nichols, 261–72. Advances in Discourse Processes 20. Norwood, NJ: Ablex, 1986.

Chaiken, Shelly. "Heuristic versus Systematic Information Processing and the Use of Source versus Message Cues in Persuasion." *Journal of Personality and Social Psychology* 39.5 (1980) 752–66.

Channell, Joanna. *Vague Language*. Oxford: Oxford University Press, 1994.

deSilva, David A. *Honor, Patronage, Kinship & Purity*. Downers Grove, IL: IVP, 2000.

________. "'Let the One Who Claims Honor Establish That Claim in the Lord': Honor Discourse in the Corinthians Correspondence." *BTB* 28 (1998) 61–74.

Dvorak, James D. "The Interpersonal Metafunction in 1 Corinthians 1–4: The Tenor of Toughness." Ph.D. diss., McMaster Divinity College, 2012.

________. "Positioning Readers with Perspective." *Perspective Criticism Blog*. http://bit.ly/1swLJX8.

________. "Thematization, Topic, and Information Flow." *Journal of the Linguistics Institute of Ancient and Biblical Greek* 1 (2008) 17–37.

Dvorak, James D., and Ryder Dale Walton. "Clause as Message: Theme, Topic, and Information Flow in Mark 2:1–12 and Jude." *BAGL* 3 (2014) 31–85.

Eagly, Alice H., and Shelly Chaiken. *Psychology of Attitudes*. Fort Worth, TX: Harcourt Brace Jovanovich, 1993.

Eggins, Suzanne. *An Introduction to Systemic Functional Linguistics*. 2nd ed. New York: Continuum, 2004.

Engberg-Pedersen, Troels. "The Gospel and Social Practice According to 1 Corinthians." *NTS* 33 (1987) 557–84.

Fairclough, Norman. *Discourse and Social Change*. Cambridge: Polity Press, 1992.

________. *Language and Power*. 3rd ed. London: Routledge, 2015.

Festinger, Leon. *A Theory of Cognitive Dissonance*. Stanford, CA: Stanford University Press, 1957.

Garland, David E. *1 Corinthians*. BECNT. Grand Rapids: Baker, 2003.

Gass, Robert H., and John S. Seiter. "Embracing Divergence: A Reexamination of Traditional and Non-traditional Conceptualizations of Persuasion." Paper presented at the Annual Convention of the Western Communication Association, Monterey, CA, November 2000.

________. *Persuasion, Social Influence, and Compliance Gaining*. 2nd ed. Boston: Allyn and Bacon, 2003.

Goatly, Andrew. *Critical Reading and Writing*. London: Routledge, 2000.

Halliday, M.A.K. *Explorations in the Functions of Language*. Explorations in Language Study. London: Arnold, 1973.

________. "The Functional Basis of Language." In *On Language and Linguistics*, edited by Jonathan J. Webster, 298–322. Collected Works of M.A.K. Halliday 3. London: Continuum, 2003.

________. *Language as Social Semiotic*. Baltimore: University Park Press, 1978.

________. "Modes of Meaning and Modes of Expression." In *On Grammar*, edited by Jonathan J. Webster, 196–218. Collected Works of M.A.K. Halliday 1. London: Continuum, 2002.

Halliday, M.A.K., and Ruqayia Hasan. *Language, Context, and Text*. Oxford: Oxford University Press, 1989.

Halliday, M.A.K., and Christian M. I. M. Matthiessen. *An Introduction to Functional Grammar*. 3rd ed. London: Arnold, 2004.

Hood, Susan. "The Persuasive Power of Prosodies: Radiating Values in Academic Writing." *Journal of English for Academic Purposes* 5 (2006) 37–49.

Hooker, Morna. "Hard Sayings: I Corinthians 3:2." *Theology* 69 (1966) 19–22.

Hudson, R.A. *Sociolinguistics*. Cambridge Textbooks of Linguistics. Cambridge: Cambridge University Press, 1980.

Hunston, Susan, and Geoff Thompson, eds. *Evaluation in Text*. Oxford: Oxford University Press, 1999.

Keener, Craig S. *A Commentary on the Gospel of Matthew*. Grand Rapids: Eerdmans, 1999.

Labov, William. "Intensity." In *Meaning, Form and Use in Context*, edited by Deborah Schiffrin, 43–70. Washington, DC: Georgetown University Press, 1984.

Lakoff, George. "Hedges: A Study in Meaning Criteria and the Logic of Fuzzy Concepts." *Journal of Philosophic Logic* 2 (1973) 458–508.

Lemke, Jay L. "Resources for Attitudinal Meaning." *Functions of Language* 5 (1998) 33–56.

________. "Semantics and Social Values." *Word* 40 (1989) 37–50.

________. *Textual Politics*. London: Taylor & Francis, 1995.

Louw, J.P., and E.A. Nida. *Greek-English Lexicon of the New Testament Based on Semantic Domains*. 2 vols. 2nd ed. New York: UBS, 1989.

Lyons, John. *Semantics*. 2 vols. Cambridge: Cambridge University Press, 1977.

Malina, Bruce J. "Authoritarianism." In *Handbook of Biblical Social Values*, edited by John J. Pilch and Bruce J. Malina, 12–19. Rev. ed. Peabody, MA: Hendrickson, 1998.

________. *Christian Origins and Cultural Anthropology*. Eugene, OR: Wipf & Stock, 2010.

Malina, Bruce J., and Jerome Neyrey. "Honor and Shame in Luke–Acts: Pivotal Values in the Mediterranean World." In *The Social World of Luke–Acts: Models for Interpretation*, edited by Jerome H. Neyrey, 25–65. Peabody, MA: Hendrickson, 1991.

Martin, J.R. "Beyond Exchange: APPRAISAL Systems in English." In *Evaluation in Text*, edited by Susan Hunston and Geoff Thompson, 142–75. Oxford: Oxford University Press, 1999.

________. *English Text: System and Structure*. Philadelphia: John Benjamins, 1992.

________. "Reading Positions/Positioning Readers." *Prospect* 10 (1995) 27–37.

________. "Text and Clause: Fractal Resonance." *Text* 15 (1995) 5–42.

Martin, J.R., and David Rose. *Genre Relations: Mapping Culture*. Equinox Textbooks and Surveys in Linguistics. London: Equinox, 2008.

Martin, J.R., and P.R.R. White. *The Language of Evaluation: Appraisal in English*. New York: Palgrave, 2005.

McVann, Mark. "Compliance." In *Handbook of Biblical Social Values*, edited by John J. Pilch and Bruce J. Malina, 33–35. Rev. ed. Peabody, MA: Hendrickson, 1998.

Meeks, Wayne A. *The Origins of Christian Morality*. New Haven: Yale University Press, 1993.

Neville, Robert C. *Reconstruction of Thinking*. Axiology of Thinking 1. New York: SUNY, 1981.

Ochs, Elinor, and Bambi Schiefflen. "Language Has a Heart." *Text* 9 (1989) 7–25.

Osiek, Carolyn. "Relatedness." In *Handbook of Biblical Social Values*, edited by John J. Pilch and Bruce J. Malina, 176–78. Rev. ed. Peabody, MA: Hendrickson, 1998.

Palmer, Frank R. *Mood and Modality*. 2nd ed. Cambridge Textbooks of Linguistics. Cambridge: Cambridge University Press, 2001.

Perelman, Chaïm, and Lucie Olbrechts-Tyteca. *The New Rhetoric: A Treatise on Argumentation*. Translated by John Wilkinson and Purcell Weaver. Notre Dame, IN: University of Notre Dame Press, 1969.

Pike, K.L. *Linguistic Concepts: An Introduction to Tagmemics*. Lincoln: University of Nebraska Press, 1982.

Pilch, John J. "Power." In *Handbook of Biblical Social Values*, edited by John J. Pilch and Bruce J. Malina, 158–61. Rev. ed. Peabody, MA: Hendrickson, 1998.

Pilch, John J., and Bruce J. Malina, eds. *Handbook of Biblical Social Values*. Rev. ed. Peabody, MA: Hendrickson, 1998.

Porter, Stanley E. *Idioms of the Greek New Testament*. 2nd ed. Biblical Languages: Greek 2. Sheffield: Sheffield Academic, 1999.

________. *Linguistic Analysis of the Greek New Testament: Studies in Tools, Methods, and Practice*. Grand Rapids: Baker Academic, 2015.

________. *Verbal Aspect in the Greek of the New Testament, with Reference to Tense and Mood*. Studies in Biblical Greek 1. New York: Peter Lang, 1993.

Poynton, Cate. *Language and Gender*. 2nd. ed. Oxford: Oxford University Press, 1989.

Reed, Jeffrey T. *A Discourse Analysis of Philippians*. JSNTSup 136. Sheffield: Sheffield Academic, 1997.

Reese, James M. "Assertiveness." In *Handbook of Biblical Social Values*, edited by John J. Pilch and Bruce J. Malina, 10–12. Rev. ed. Peabody, MA: Hendrickson, 1998.

Theissen, Gerd. "Social Stratification in the Corinthians Community: A Contribution to the Sociology of Early Hellenistic Christianity." In *The Social Setting of Pauling Christianity*, edited by John H. Schütz, 69–119. Philadelphia: Fortress, 1982.

Thiselton, Anthony C. *The First Epistle to the Corinthians*. NIGTC. Grand Rapids: Eerdmans, 2000.

Thompson, Geoff, and Susan Hunston. "Evaluation: An Introduction." In *Evaluation in Text*, edited by Susan Hunston and Geoff Thompson, 1–27. Oxford: Oxford University Press, 1999.

Tucker, J. Brian. *You Belong to Christ: Paul and the Formation of Social Identity in 1 Corinthians 1–4*. Eugene, OR: Pickwick, 2010.

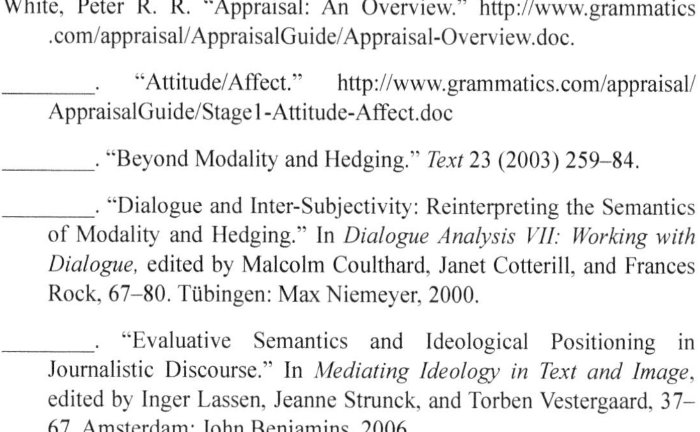

White, Peter R. R. "Appraisal: An Overview." http://www.grammatics.com/appraisal/AppraisalGuide/Appraisal-Overview.doc.

________. "Attitude/Affect." http://www.grammatics.com/appraisal/AppraisalGuide/Stage1-Attitude-Affect.doc

________. "Beyond Modality and Hedging." *Text* 23 (2003) 259–84.

________. "Dialogue and Inter-Subjectivity: Reinterpreting the Semantics of Modality and Hedging." In *Dialogue Analysis VII: Working with Dialogue,* edited by Malcolm Coulthard, Janet Cotterill, and Frances Rock, 67–80. Tübingen: Max Niemeyer, 2000.

________. "Evaluative Semantics and Ideological Positioning in Journalistic Discourse." In *Mediating Ideology in Text and Image*, edited by Inger Lassen, Jeanne Strunck, and Torben Vestergaard, 37–67. Amsterdam: John Benjamins, 2006.

Ancient Sources Index

Old Testament

Apocrypha

New Testament

Greco-Roman Writings

Inscriptions

Modern Authors Index

www.ingramcontent.com/pod-product-compliance
Ingram Content Group UK Ltd.
Pitfield, Milton Keynes, MK11 3LW, UK
UKHW020134250726
13967UKWH00002B/649

9 781498 295444